Why The Future Belongs To Us

A Vision of Hope, Healing, and
Unlimited Possibility for Black America

By
Coach Michael Taylor

Why The Future Belongs To Us
A Vision of Hope, Healing, and Unlimited Possibilities For Black America

Published by Creation Publishing Group LLC
www.creationpublishing.com
©2026 by Michael Taylor
ISBN # 979-8-9988491-3-8
Library of Congress Number # 2025927061

Cover design by Rebecacovers on Fiverr
Photo by Penda Kamati on Pexel

Published and printed in the United States of America.

DEDICATION

This book is dedicated to every Black man, woman, and child
who has ever been told who they were
before they had the chance to discover it for themselves.

To the ones who carried burdens that weren't theirs,
who inherited fears that weren't born in them,
who survived stories they did not choose
and still found a way to rise,
to love,
to dream,
to believe.

May these pages remind you of the truth:
you are more powerful than your past,
more brilliant than your circumstances,
and more necessary to the future
than you've ever been taught to believe.

To our ancestors —
who endured the unendurable,
who dreamed the impossible,
who held on to hope when hope had no evidence.
Your courage is the foundation upon which this book stands.

To the future generations —
may you inherit not our wounds,
but our wisdom;
not our fears,
but our freedom;
not our limitations,
but our limitless possibility.

And to my beloved wife, **Bedra** —
your love, your strength, and your unwavering belief in me
are the wind behind every word I write.
Thank you for walking beside me
as we build a future worth dreaming about.

ACKNOWLEDGMENTS

First and foremost, I acknowledge **Divine Intelligence** — the eternal source of wisdom, insight, inspiration, and guidance that breathed this book into existence. Every word was shaped by a Presence greater than myself, and I offer my deepest gratitude for being chosen as a vessel for its message.

I honor **Dr. Martin Luther King Jr.**, whose prophetic voice still echoes across generations. His dream was not a metaphor, it was a blueprint. His courage was not an anomaly, it was a calling. His legacy continues to light the path toward the future we are now stepping into.

I acknowledge **Colin Kaepernick**, whose bravery reminded the world that silence is complicity and that one person, rooted in truth, can shake the conscience of a nation. His stand, taken on one knee, awakened millions.

I honor **Trayvon Martin**, whose life was stolen far too soon. His name became a catalyst for awakening, stirring a movement that continues to demand accountability, humanity, and justice.

I honor **George Floyd**, whose final breaths shook the world from complacency.

Killed in 2020 in Minneapolis when an officer knelt on his neck for more than nine minutes, his death sparked one of the largest global protest movements in human history. His life changed the world.

I honor **Eric Garner**, who died in 2014 in Staten Island after being placed in a banned chokehold, gasping the words, *"I can't breathe."* His final plea became a rallying cry for justice movements everywhere.

I honor **Michael Brown**, fatally shot in 2014 in Ferguson, Missouri. His death ignited nationwide protests and exposed the militarization of policing in America, forcing the world to witness the realities Black communities have long faced.

I honor **Tamir Rice**, a 12-year-old child whose life was taken within seconds of police arriving on the scene in 2014. His name continues to call for reform, accountability, and the protection of our children.

I honor **Philando Castile**, killed in 2016 during a traffic stop in Falcon Heights, Minnesota. The world watched the aftermath in real time, and it forever changed the national conversation about bias, policing, and the vulnerability of Black lives.

To each of these men and boys —
You were more than news headlines.
You were sons, fathers, brothers, friends, and human beings.
Your lives mattered.
Your names matter.
Your legacy matters.

This book is a testament to the world you deserved, and the world we are still committed to building.

Finally, I acknowledge the love of my life, **my wife, Bedra**. Your unwavering support, your wisdom, your strength, and your belief in me ground every project I create. You are my partner in purpose, my anchor in truth, and my greatest blessing. Thank you for standing with me, dreaming with me, and walking this sacred path by my side.

TABLE OF CONTENTS

PROLOGUE

The Moment I Realized the Future Was Still Ours

I didn't arrive at optimism because life made it easy.
I arrived there because life demanded it.

There was a moment, a quiet, unremarkable moment on the surface, when everything I thought I knew about being a Black man in America collapsed in on itself. It didn't happen during a protest or after a powerful speech. It didn't happen in a church pew or a therapy session. It happened alone, in a room no bigger than my doubts, on a night when I was exhausted by carrying the weight of a story that wasn't mine to hold anymore.

For years, like so many of us, I'd been taught to see the world through the lens of caution, survival, and inherited fear. I learned to shrink my possibilities so the world wouldn't feel threatened by them. I learned to brace myself for disappointment just in case hope turned out to be too heavy. I learned to anticipate rejection, injustice, and bias, long before they ever arrived.

But on that night, something unexpected happened.

It wasn't a voice from the heavens.
It wasn't a lightning strike.
It wasn't a dramatic vision.

It was a whisper, quiet, steady, undeniable.
A knowing that rose up from a place deeper than thought, deeper than memory, deeper than fear.

It said:

"What if the story you've been told about being Black in America is too small for who you really are?"

I sat with that question for a long time.

Because somewhere inside me, beneath the layers of cultural conditioning and historical trauma, beneath the stereotypes and survival strategies, beneath the pain and the pride, something began to awaken. Something ancient. Something powerful. Something free.

It was the awareness that my life, and our collective life, did not have to be shaped by the shadows of the past…
but could instead be shaped by the possibilities of the future.

It was the awareness that I had been taught to fear a world that was actually evolving.
That I had been prepared to survive in a world that no longer existed.
That I had inherited beliefs formed in a different era, beliefs that no longer served me, no longer fit me, no longer reflected the truth of my experience.

It was the moment I realized that the narrative I had been handed was not the narrative I had to continue living.

The fear wasn't mine.
The limits weren't mine.
The doubt wasn't mine.
The pessimism wasn't mine.

And if it wasn't mine…
I could let it go.

That realization didn't erase injustice.
It didn't rewrite history.
It didn't magically fix the systems around me.

But it did something far more important:

It freed my mind.
It expanded my vision.
It gave me permission to imagine without inherited fear.

It allowed me to see that Black America was not doomed we were transforming.

In that moment, I saw something clearly for the first time:

Our future is not defined by what we've endured.
It is defined by what we are becoming.

And we are becoming extraordinary.

We are healing.
We are creating.
We are learning.
We are leading.
We are awakening.
We are uniting.
We are rising from the inside out.

This book was born from that moment,
the moment I stopped letting the past predict our path
and started trusting the brilliance, resilience, and spiritual power of
who we truly are.

If you turn these pages with an open heart, you will see what I saw that night:

The future does not belong to those who fear.
The future belongs to those who believe.

And make no mistake about it
the future belongs to us.

INTRODUCTION: A NEW NARRATIVE FOR A NEW ERA

We are living in a moment of profound transition.

The old stories that once defined identity, power, and possibility are losing their grip. They no longer explain the world as it is becoming, and they no longer serve the people who are ready to move forward. Across culture, politics, education, and consciousness itself, something is shifting. The questions people are asking today are no longer about whether change is necessary, but about who we must become to sustain it.

This book was born from that evolution.

It emerged from a recognition that Black America is not standing still, waiting for permission or validation. We are thinking differently. Healing differently. Creating differently. Leading differently. And most importantly, seeing ourselves differently. The internal narratives that once shaped identity through limitation, survival, and reaction are being questioned, interrupted, and rewritten.

This book is written first and foremost for Black people who are ready to move from survival into authorship.

It is for those who sense, even quietly, that something deeper is happening within themselves and within the collective. For those who feel less interested in explaining the past and more committed to shaping the future. For those who understand that while history matters, it does not get to have the final word.

At the same time, this book welcomes any reader who is willing to engage these ideas with openness, humility, and respect. Anyone who believes that human potential expands when truth is named, consciousness evolves, and agency is reclaimed will find themselves reflected somewhere in these pages.

What follows is not a denial of history, pain, or injustice. It is an expansion beyond them. This book does not ask you to forget what has happened. It asks you to consider what is now possible when identity is no longer organized around damage, but around capacity.

Throughout these chapters, we will examine belief systems that have shaped perception and behavior, both externally and internally. We will explore how inherited narratives can quietly limit imagination, and how releasing them creates space for growth. We will look honestly at the forces that have influenced Black identity while refusing to allow those forces to define its future.

This is not a book about blame.
It is a book about responsibility.

Not responsibility as burden, but responsibility as authorship.

Because when a people understand that they are not merely reacting to the world, but actively creating it, everything changes. Choices become intentional. Healing becomes strategic. Creativity becomes foundational. The future stops feeling abstract and begins to feel participatory.

The chapters ahead are offered as reflections, invitations, and frameworks for that participation. They are meant to be read slowly, revisited often, and engaged with honestly. There is no single correct way to move through this book. There is only the question of what resonates, and what you are ready to carry forward.

We are not at the end of a story.
We are at the threshold of a new one.

And the future will be shaped by those who are willing to claim authorship over who they are becoming.

"The most potent weapon in the hands of the oppressor is the mind of the oppressed."

— **Steve Biko**

CHAPTER 1

WHAT IS THE CWBS?

Understanding the Invisible Belief System That Shaped America

I've spent most of my adult life trying to understand why people believe what they believe. Not just Black people. Not just white people. Human beings. We like to think our beliefs are logical, rational, or rooted in truth, but most of what we believe about the world comes from sources we never consciously chose. Our families. Our neighborhoods. Our schools. The media we consumed before we were old enough to ask questions. The stories we absorbed before we even knew we were listening.

If we're honest, much of what we think is "our belief" is really someone else's programming.

When I first began examining stereotypes and race relations, I realized something most people never consider: beliefs are inherited long before they are questioned. They are absorbed before they are examined. They are adopted before they are understood. This is why I came to define something I call **The Collective White Belief System**, or **CWBS**—a powerful, unconscious set of ideas that shaped America's earliest identity and still influences subtle attitudes today.

To understand the future of Black America, we must first understand the system that shaped so much of the past.

Not to blame.
Not to shame.
But to see clearly.

Because you cannot transform something you refuse to name.

5

THE UNSEEN ARCHITECTURE OF BELIEF

The best way to explain the CWBS is to imagine a house built hundreds of years ago. The people living in it today didn't pour the foundation, didn't draw the blueprints, and didn't decide what the structure would look like. They simply inherited it. They were born into rooms they didn't design, hallways they didn't choose, and windows that frame the world in a particular way.

The CWBS is that house.

It was constructed during a time when white supremacy wasn't a fringe idea, it was the organizing principle of an entire society. It was written into laws, reinforced through religion, justified by science, and embedded into every institution that shaped early American life. And because these beliefs were repeated generation after generation, they became normalized. Invisible. "Just the way things are."

A child raised inside that house didn't wake up one day and say, "I choose to believe in racial hierarchy."
No, the belief was already there, quietly handed down like family heirlooms.

Most white people today are not consciously racist, hateful, or malicious. In fact, many are actively working to build a more just and equitable world. But they still may carry remnants of a belief system they never chose, one they inherited through cultural osmosis.

The CWBS is not about conscious intent.
It's about subconscious inheritance.

And that distinction is critical if we are going to build bridges rather than walls.

THE PSYCHOLOGY OF INHERITANCE

Human beings are born without beliefs, just like a brand-new computer with an empty hard drive. The operating system gets installed through repetition and reinforcement. Parents upload their beliefs. Schools upload their beliefs. Media uploads its beliefs. Society uploads its beliefs. By the time a child becomes an adult, their subconscious mind is filled with programs they never consciously approved—but they run anyway.

If you were born in America—regardless of race—you inherited ideas about race you did not ask for.

White children inherited the belief that whiteness is the norm, the standard, the center of the story.
Black children inherited beliefs about their identity shaped by the distortions of the dominant culture.

No one chose this system.

We were all drafted into it without our consent.

But the good news, the beautiful news, and the reason this book exists is that **belief systems evolve**. They change as consciousness changes. They dissolve as awareness expands. They lose their power as truth replaces illusion.

And right now, America is undergoing one of the greatest consciousness shifts in its history.

What makes inherited belief systems so powerful is that they rarely announce themselves. They operate quietly, beneath awareness, shaping perception long before reason has a chance to intervene. Most people do not wake up and consciously choose the assumptions they hold about race, intelligence, beauty, danger, or worth. Those assumptions arrive prepackaged, reinforced by repetition and normalized through familiarity.

This is why conversations about race often feel emotionally charged even when facts are presented calmly. When a belief is challenged, the mind does not experience it as an intellectual disagreement.

It experiences it as a threat to identity. The subconscious reacts defensively because it is protecting the internal architecture that has provided a sense of order, even if that order was built on distortion.

Understanding this helps us move beyond blame and into insight.

If belief systems are inherited, then awakening is not about accusation. It is about interruption. It is about pausing long enough to ask, "Where did this idea come from?" and "Does this belief still serve truth, justice, or humanity?" That pause is the beginning of liberation.

When people begin questioning beliefs they did not choose, consciousness expands. And when enough individuals begin questioning at the same time, culture begins to shift.

This is exactly what we are witnessing now.

WHY MOST WHITE PEOPLE TODAY ARE NOT RACIST

This is an uncomfortable truth for some people to accept because so much of our public dialogue is built on conflict and accusation. But the reality is simple: the majority of white Americans today are not consciously racist. Many want genuine connection. Many want understanding. Many want to dismantle the very systems their ancestors benefited from.

Every generation becomes less prejudiced.
Less defensive.
Less programmed by the CWBS.

Why?
Because belief systems weaken when they stop being reinforced.

Younger white Americans are growing up in a different world. Their classrooms are diverse. Their heroes are diverse. Their media consumption is global. Their friendships cross racial lines in ways unimaginable 50 years ago. Many of them reject the old narratives not because they were taught to, but because those narratives no longer make sense in the world they inhabit.

The CWBS is dissolving.
Not overnight.
Not perfectly.
But undeniably.

This is one of the great reasons to be optimistic about the future of Black America.

Because racial harmony isn't just possible, it's already happening in millions of quiet, everyday interactions that never make the news.

Another reason optimism is warranted is that belief systems do not survive exposure. The CWBS thrived in isolation, in homogeneous communities, and in tightly controlled narratives. Today's world offers far less insulation. People are exposed to different cultures, stories, and perspectives earlier in life and with greater frequency than ever before.

Exposure humanizes.

It becomes increasingly difficult to maintain abstract fears when real relationships exist. It becomes harder to cling to inherited narratives when lived experience contradicts them. This is why proximity matters. Not proximity as performance, but proximity as genuine relationship.

The more people know one another as individuals, the less power stereotypes hold.

This does not mean prejudice has vanished, nor does it mean progress is linear. It means the conditions that once sustained the CWBS are eroding. And systems that depend on insulation cannot survive in an interconnected world.

Change does not always arrive as dramatic revolution. Sometimes it arrives quietly, through friendships, families, workplaces, classrooms, and communities where old assumptions simply no longer fit reality.

That kind of change is slower, but it is far more durable.

HOW THE CWBS SHAPED THE BLACK EXPERIENCE

Understanding the CWBS is not about excusing racial injustice. It's about understanding the forces that shaped the false narratives we've lived under for centuries.

The CWBS created the stereotypes.
The CWBS created the lies about Black intelligence, morality, and potential.
The CWBS shaped the criminal justice system, housing patterns, economic disparities, and educational inequities.

But here's the truth many people overlook:

Even under the weight of the CWBS, Black Americans have built families, culture, innovation, spirituality, entrepreneurship, education, science, activism, and art that continue to influence the entire world.

The CWBS tried to define us—but it could never contain us.

And now that the CWBS is crumbling, Black America stands at a powerful threshold: to see ourselves through our own eyes, not through the distorted lens of a fading belief system.

The future belongs to those who release the false narratives of the past.

HUMAN EVOLUTION: THE REAL STORY BEHIND RACE RELATIONS

The greatest shift happening today isn't political—it's psychological. It's spiritual. It's evolutionary. Human beings are waking up. They're questioning inherited beliefs. They're challenging assumptions. They're recognizing the humanity in one another in ways that were not possible in earlier generations.

This is not accidental.
This is consciousness evolving.

Every major spiritual tradition has said the same thing in different ways:

We are here to awaken.
We are here to grow.
We are here to evolve beyond fear and separation.

Racism is not just a social issue—it is a symptom of unawakened consciousness. It is the byproduct of fear, insecurity, and inherited programming. And as awareness expands, racism loses its fuel source.

We are witnessing the slow but undeniable emergence of a more conscious America. One that sees through the illusion of racial hierarchy. One that understands the interconnectedness of all human beings. One that recognizes the beauty, brilliance, and potential of Black people without needing to filter it through guilt, fear, or ignorance.

This is not wishful thinking.
This is observable reality.

The old world is dying.
A new one is emerging.

And Black America is positioned to thrive in ways our ancestors could only dream of.

THE GIFT OF UNDERSTANDING THE CWBS

When you understand the CWBS, you stop taking racism personally. You stop absorbing someone else's projections. You stop internalizing the limitations others try to place on you. You no longer see yourself through the mirror of someone else's unconscious programming.

You see clearly.
You see truthfully.
You see with wisdom rather than reaction.

Understanding the CWBS gives you power.

Power to choose your beliefs.
Power to reclaim your identity.
Power to define your future.
Power to see that racism's grip is weakening—not strengthening.
Power to recognize that the world is shifting in ways that favor expansion, not oppression.

And most importantly…

It gives you the power to approach the future with optimism.

Because once you understand the CWBS, you also understand that it is not eternal. It is not fixed. It is not a permanent structure in the human psyche. It is already dissolving through:

- education

- exposure

- empathy

- diversity

- interracial relationships

- cultural exchange

- spiritual awakening

- the evolution of human consciousness

Humans are not who we were 50 years ago.
We are not even who we were 15 years ago.

And we won't be the same 15 years from now.

Consciousness is rising.
The story is shifting.
The future is unfolding in our favor.

There is another dimension to this conversation that deserves attention, especially for Black readers who have carried the weight of misrepresentation for generations.

When you understand the CWBS, you begin to recognize that many of the limitations placed on Black identity were never reflections of truth. They were reflections of fear. Fear of difference. Fear of loss of dominance. Fear of having to share space, power, and narrative authority.

Seen through this lens, the stereotypes lose their sting. Not because they were harmless, but because they are revealed as projections rather than realities. And when projections are exposed, they lose their authority.

This understanding allows a profound shift to occur internally.

Instead of reacting to every instance of ignorance or bias, you begin to move with discernment. You stop allowing outdated narratives to dictate your emotional state or self-concept. You begin to see yourself not as someone struggling against history, but as someone standing at the forefront of a new chapter in human evolution.

That shift is subtle, but it is transformative.

It replaces defensiveness with clarity.
It replaces anger with discernment.
It replaces despair with grounded optimism.

And it prepares the mind for what comes next.

CLOSING: THE FOUNDATION FOR A NEW NARRATIVE

This chapter is not about assigning blame.
It's not about guilt.
It's not about dwelling in the past.

It's about clarity.

When we see the CWBS for what it is—an inherited, outdated, dissolving belief system—we free ourselves to build something new. We free ourselves to rewrite our identity. We free ourselves to unlearn the lies that were never ours to carry. And we free ourselves to imagine a future not defined by trauma, but by possibility.

This book begins here because liberation begins in the mind.
When we understand the beliefs that shaped America, we are finally free to create the nation—and the future, we deserve.

The CWBS may have shaped the past.
But it has no authority over our future.

The future belongs to us.

And now that we understand where the old story came from,
we are ready to write a new one.

And yet, even as we acknowledge the dissolution of the old belief system, it's important to understand that this moment in history is more than a sociological shift. It's a spiritual inflection point. Human consciousness evolves the same way individuals evolve: through pressure, through contrast, through discomfort, and through awakening. In the same way your personal life challenges forced you to grow, refine your beliefs, and deepen your understanding of your own identity, humanity as a collective is experiencing a similar process.

Every era of great change is preceded by an era of great turbulence. We are living through the turbulence now. The arguments on social media, the political polarization, the cultural friction — all of this is evidence that the old world is trying to hold on while the new world is already being born. When belief systems crumble, they do not go quietly. They shake, they resist, they protest. But their collapse is inevitable because evolution never moves backward.

In this sense, the decline of the CWBS is not just a cultural moment — it is a chapter in the unfolding story of human awakening. It means that more people are beginning to think for themselves instead of simply absorbing the beliefs of generations past. It means that empathy is expanding. It means that the human heart is opening. And it means that the lies that once justified inequality cannot survive the light of awareness that now exists.

The beauty of this moment is that Black America stands at the intersection of history and possibility. We are the inheritors of a legacy of unimaginable resilience. We are the descendants of people who endured the worst and still created the best. Music. Culture. Spirituality. Innovation. Faith. Vision. These gifts were forged in fire, and now they are ready to shine in ways the world has never seen.

When an old belief system dies, new identities become possible. New stories become possible. New futures become possible. And that is the opportunity before us now. The question is no longer "What happened to us?" or "What did America do to us?" The question is, "Who do we choose to become now that nothing is holding us back but the beliefs we carry within ourselves?"

Understanding the CWBS allows us to release the fear that someone else's perception can control our destiny. It reminds us that the greatest power we will ever hold is the power to define ourselves. It invites us to stand in the truth of our brilliance, our creativity, our strength, and our spiritual sovereignty. And most importantly, it sets the stage for a new kind of optimism — an optimism based not on denial, but on awareness; not on fantasy, but on truth; not on hope alone, but on evidence that the world is changing in our favor.

This is the moment our ancestors prayed for. This is the moment they dreamed of when they sang spirituals under the night sky, imagining a day when their descendants would walk freely, think freely, and live fully. We are living out their prophecy. We are carrying the torch they lit. And now that the weight of the old belief system is fading, the brilliance of who we truly are can finally be seen without distortion.

The CWBS may have framed the past, but we are framing the future. And that future is vast, expansive, and filled with possibility. Because once you understand the forces that shaped the old narrative, you are no longer bound by it. You become the author of the new one — and that is where our power resides.

At its core, this chapter is an invitation to maturity. It asks us to move beyond simplistic good versus evil frameworks and into a more nuanced understanding of how belief systems operate across generations. It challenges us to see racism not only as a moral failing, but as a developmental one. A stage of consciousness that humanity is now outgrowing.

This does not minimize the harm caused. It contextualizes it.

Growth requires honesty, and honesty requires courage. It takes courage to examine the invisible structures that shaped a nation. It takes courage to acknowledge how deeply those structures influenced us all. And it takes even greater courage to believe that transformation is possible.

But history shows us that evolution is relentless. Humanity has outgrown countless belief systems that once seemed permanent. Monarchies, slavery, religious absolutism, and rigid social hierarchies all appeared immutable in their time. None survived the expansion of consciousness.

The CWBS will be no different.

Understanding this does not make us passive. It makes us precise. It allows us to participate in change without being consumed by it. It allows us to focus energy on creation rather than reaction. And it allows us to step into the future with a confidence rooted not in fantasy, but in pattern recognition.

Systems rise. Systems fall. Consciousness expands.

And those who understand this are always positioned to thrive.

"You don't have to accept the roles other people give you."

— **James Baldwin**

CHAPTER 2

THE "THAT'S WHAT WHITE PEOPLE DO" MENTALITY

Breaking Free from Internal Limits and Reclaiming Our Power

One of the most fascinating things I've observed over the past thirty years of speaking, coaching, and listening to Black folks across America is how deeply our internal belief systems shape our sense of possibility. We often talk about the stereotypes others place on us, but we sometimes avoid confronting the subtle stereotypes we place on *ourselves*. Not the loud ones. Not the outward ones. The quiet ones we don't even realize we're carrying. The ones we inherited the same way others inherited the CWBS — through repetition, environment, and cultural norms that seeped into our subconscious before we were old enough to question them.

Among those subtle beliefs is a phrase I've heard spoken in barbershops, family gatherings, school hallways, workspaces, social media threads, and casual conversations:
"That's what white people do."

It's usually said jokingly. Sometimes with humor, sometimes with pride, and sometimes with a hint of resignation. But underneath the humor lies something deeper — an invisible boundary, a quiet suggestion that certain behaviors, opportunities, and aspirations belong to white people, and not to us. It might sound harmless on the surface, but like all internalized beliefs, it carries weight. It shapes identity. It influences decisions. And when repeated often enough, it creates an unconscious ceiling that sits just above our dreams.

The truth is, many of us grew up internalizing limits we never consciously agreed to. Limits handed down through generational trauma. Limits shaped by media portrayals. Limits we absorbed by watching how society treated our parents, our uncles, our aunts, our neighbors. Limits formed by the ongoing remnants of a world struggling to evolve beyond its own outdated thinking. And whether we knew it or not, those limits found a home in the deepest corners of our psyche.

That's why this chapter is necessary. Because if Chapter 1 revealed the belief system white Americans inherited, Chapter 2 reveals the belief system many Black Americans inherited. Not out of weakness. Not out of ignorance. But out of survival.

But survival is not the same as thriving.

And now we stand in a moment where thriving is not just possible — it's calling us forward.

There is something important to understand about moments like this in history. They are not random. They arrive when internal readiness finally meets external opportunity. For generations, Black people carried ambition without access, vision without infrastructure, and potential without permission. That disconnect created frustration, not because we lacked ability, but because the world had not yet caught up to our capacity.

Today, that mismatch is shrinking.

We are living in an era where access to information is no longer gatekept. Where learning is no longer confined to institutions that were never designed with us in mind. Where creativity can become capital, ideas can become enterprises, and voices can travel globally without waiting for validation. This shift does not erase history, but it does change what is required of us now.

Thriving asks something different than surviving.

It asks us to examine not only what was done to us, but what we are now willing to do for ourselves.

THE QUIET POWER OF INTERNAL NARRATIVES

We all have a voice inside our heads that narrates our lives. Sometimes it whispers. Sometimes it shouts. Sometimes it guides us. And sometimes it undermines us. That internal narrator begins building its vocabulary long before we are conscious of it. It learns from what we see, what we hear, and what we experience.

For far too many Black folks, that narrator learned early on to differentiate between what "we" do and what "white people" do. As if ambition had a race. As if curiosity had a color. As if exploration, travel, education, risk-taking, or dreaming belonged to one group but not another.

And why wouldn't we internalize this message when we were constantly shown images suggesting that whiteness occupied the center of everything? For generations, white people were portrayed as the explorers, the entrepreneurs, the scientists, the CEOs, the writers, the climbers, the meditators, the minimalists, the ranch owners, the world travelers. Meanwhile, Black people were often confined to narrow portrayals that reinforced limitation rather than possibility.

Even if we consciously rejected those portrayals, they left residue. They created a subconscious divide between what "they" can do and what "we" should expect for ourselves.

But here's the truth: that divide never actually existed. It was manufactured by a society that had not yet awakened to the truth of our brilliance.

And once we see through the illusion, we can never unsee it.

Internal narratives do not simply influence what we believe. They influence what we notice. When the mind accepts a belief about what is possible, it filters reality to confirm it. Opportunities that fall outside that belief often go unseen, dismissed before they are even consciously evaluated.

This is why two people can stand in the same environment and experience completely different worlds.

One sees obstacles everywhere.
The other sees openings.

The difference is not intelligence or effort. It is belief.

When a person believes something is "not for them," the mind quietly stops scanning for evidence to the contrary. Over time, this becomes self-reinforcing. The absence of evidence feels like confirmation, even when the absence is self-created.

Breaking this cycle requires awareness before action. You cannot choose differently until you see differently. And you cannot see differently until you question the narrator that has been speaking in your head for most of your life.

That questioning is not rebellion.
It is maturity.

HOW LIMITING BELIEFS GET PASSED DOWN

People sometimes assume limiting beliefs come from ignorance, but most limiting beliefs come from love. They're passed down by parents who want to protect us. By communities trying to shield us from disappointment. By family members who watched someone try and fail and didn't want us to feel the same pain. By elders who lived through eras where the risks we now take freely were simply not safe for them to attempt.

What sounded like caution was often trauma speaking. What sounded like wisdom was sometimes fear wearing a mask. What sounded like guidance was often a survival strategy passed down from those who had no other choice.

When a grandmother tells her grandson not to trust the system, she isn't planting negativity — she's recalling a lifetime of systemic harm. When a father tells his daughter to "be realistic," he isn't doubting her potential — he's trying to protect her from heartbreak in a world he learned to navigate with armor. When a young Black man says, "That's what white people do," he may be joking, but the joke didn't originate in humor. It originated in the belief that certain doors historically weren't open to us.

But here's the irony: while these beliefs once served as armor, today they act as anchors.

We are living in a different world than the one our grandparents survived. The opportunities available to us today would have been unthinkable in their lifetime. Technology has leveled the playing field. Information is universal. Creativity is currency. Entrepreneurship is accessible. And most importantly, consciousness is evolving.

The armor that once protected us is now too heavy to wear.

It's time to put it down.

There is a moment many Black adults experience, often in their thirties or forties, when they suddenly realize that some of the advice they were given as children no longer applies to the world they live in now. The rules have changed, but the internal operating system has not yet updated.

This realization can feel disorienting at first.

You begin to notice how often caution overrides curiosity. How quickly you talk yourself out of ideas that excite you. How familiar phrases surface in moments of ambition, even when there is no external threat present. These are not personal failures. They are signs of outdated programming still running quietly in the background.

The work, then, is not to shame ourselves for carrying these beliefs, but to thank them for the role they once played and then consciously release them. Gratitude allows letting go without resentment. And letting go creates space.

Space for new ideas.
Space for new identities.
Space for a future that does not resemble the past.

THE DANGER OF INVISIBLE BOUNDARIES

Every time we say, "That's what white people do," a boundary gets reinforced. We may not feel it. We may not notice it. But the psyche does. The mind hears it as a command:
"Stay in your lane. Don't dream too big. Don't imagine yourself there."

These unconscious boundaries don't just shape individual choices. They shape the identity of a community. They influence what we attempt, what we avoid, what we pursue, and what we believe is possible. They can make us second-guess our desires or dismiss them altogether.

Want to start a vineyard? That's what white people do.
Want to climb mountains? That's what white people do.
Want to backpack across Europe? That's what white people do.
Want to open a tech startup? That's what white people do.
Want to meditate? Journal? Explore Buddhism? Invest in stocks?
Buy a ranch? That's what white people do.

But who decided this?
Where did these invisible rules come from?
And more importantly… why are we still obeying them?

The answer is simple: because no one ever told us the game had changed.

And that is what this book exists to do — to tell the truth about who we really are, what we're capable of, and why the future belongs to us.

RECLAIMING OUR FULL RANGE OF HUMANITY

Human beings have an innate desire to explore, create, innovate, question, and grow. None of these impulses belong to a race. They belong to the human spirit. But once you've been conditioned to believe the world has placed you in a box, you begin to shrink yourself to fit inside it.

Breaking free from the "That's what white people do" mentality is not about doing things because white people do them. It's about reclaiming the full range of our humanity — the parts of ourselves we were never given permission to explore.

We meditate because our spirits need stillness.
We travel because our souls crave expansion.
We innovate because our minds are brilliant.
We write because our stories matter.
We build businesses because entrepreneurship is in our blood.
We heal because healing is our birthright.
We dream because we were born to.

Many of the things we labeled as "white" were never white — they were universal. We were simply denied access to them for so long that we forgot they belonged to us too.

The future requires us to remember.

Reclaiming humanity also means reclaiming nuance. It means allowing ourselves to be complex, contradictory, and evolving. It means resisting the urge to perform identity in ways that feel familiar but limiting.

Blackness has never been one thing. It has always contained multitudes. The problem was never our diversity. The problem was the narrow lens through which we were allowed to be seen.

As that lens widens, so does permission.

Permission to rest.
Permission to explore.
Permission to fail and try again.
Permission to pursue paths without precedent.

And perhaps most importantly, permission to succeed without apology.

When Black people give themselves this permission, something profound shifts. Identity becomes expansive rather than defensive. Life becomes exploratory rather than reactive. And the future begins to feel less like a distant promise and more like a present invitation.

WHY TAKING RESPONSIBILITY IS THE ULTIMATE ACT OF LIBERATION

Some people hear the word "responsibility" and mistake it for blame. But responsibility is not blame, it is *power.* Responsibility means we are not waiting for external forces to fix our lives. It means we understand that the beliefs we carry shape the world we experience. It means we stop letting society decide what is possible for us. It means we refuse to shrink in the presence of our own potential.

Taking responsibility for our beliefs is the most revolutionary thing a Black person can do.

Because once you reclaim your belief system, you reclaim your life.

And once a community reclaims its belief system, it reclaims its future.

A NEW IDENTITY IS EMERGING

There is a new energy rising within Black America. I feel it every time I speak at an HBCU. I feel it in the emails I receive from young Black professionals. I feel it in the entrepreneurs' building companies from their laptops. I feel it in the spiritual communities seeking truth beyond tradition. I feel it in the artists, the creators, the healers, the thinkers, the activists, and the everyday dreamers quietly reshaping the narrative of what it means to be Black in the 21st century.

This new identity is not reactive.
It is not defined by trauma.
It is not limited by history.
It is not boxed in by stereotypes.

It is expansive.
It is visionary.
It is empowered.
It is free.

It says:
"I define me. I choose my path. I write my story."

That is the energy that will carry Black America into the future.

CLOSING: A CALL TO STEP INTO OUR FULL POWER

Saying "That's what white people do" was once a shield. A coping mechanism. A way to navigate a world that told us certain things weren't meant for us. But today, those words no longer protect us, they imprison us. They shrink our horizons. They clip our wings.

The truth is, there is nothing on this earth that is off-limits to us.
Not success.
Not happiness.
Not joy.
Not wealth.

Not wellness.
Not exploration.
Not creativity.
Not rest.
Not abundance.
Not wonder.
Not purpose.

Everything the world offers belongs to us too.

Our ancestors fought too hard.
Suffered too much.
Sacrificed too deeply.
Dreamed too boldly.

For us to live small.

The future will not be built by those who hide from their potential.
The future will be built by those who embrace it.

The "That's what white people do" mentality is dying.
A new mentality is rising.

And that new mentality says:
We can do anything.
We can be anything.
We can create anything.
We can imagine anything.
We can claim everything.

This is where our power begins.

This is where our story transforms.

And this is where the future — our future — truly starts to unfold.

It is also important to acknowledge that unlearning internalized limits can create discomfort within our own communities. When someone steps outside familiar boundaries, it can challenge the shared assumptions that once created belonging. Growth often disrupts comfort before it creates new stability.

This does not mean growth is betrayal.

It means transformation requires renegotiation.

As more Black people step into spaces once labeled as "not for us," the culture itself begins to stretch. New norms form. New reference points emerge. And what once felt exceptional gradually becomes ordinary.

That is how cultural evolution works.

The first person is questioned.
The second is tolerated.
The third is accepted.
The fourth is expected.

And eventually, the boundary disappears altogether.

And yet, even as we step into this new identity, it's important to recognize that unlearning is a process. We don't shed limiting beliefs all at once. We peel them away layer by layer, the same way we peel away habits that no longer serve us. Some of these beliefs were woven into our childhoods before we even understood their implications. Others were absorbed through the media, through observations, through warnings whispered out of love. They became the background noise of our identity, always there, even when we weren't consciously listening.

That's why true liberation requires patience. Not because transformation is slow, but because awareness takes time to settle in. We have to learn how to trust our own potential again. We have to learn how to see ourselves without the shadow of inherited limits. We have to learn how to dream without fear of being punished for it. And we have to learn how to imagine ourselves doing things no one in our family or community ever did before, not because they couldn't, but because history didn't give them the space.

One of the greatest acts of freedom we can practice is allowing ourselves to step into spaces our ancestors could only envision. When we take risks they were denied, we honor them. When we break patterns that once kept our families safe but now hold us back, we evolve their legacy. When we embrace new experiences, new identities, and new possibilities, we are not abandoning our roots, we are expanding them.

And the beautiful thing about expansion is that it doesn't just change us; it changes everyone who witnesses us. Every Black person who climbs a mountain inspires another to explore. Every Black entrepreneur who builds a business plants a seed in the mind of a child watching quietly from the sidelines. Every Black meditator, traveler, scientist, farmer, filmmaker, tech founder, or minimalist gently dissolves the illusion that identity has boundaries. We become living proof that the story is changing. That the narrative is shifting. That the limits we once placed on ourselves were never real to begin with.

In this way, liberation becomes contagious. When one of us steps into a new possibility, it creates a ripple effect that touches everyone around us. People start to question their assumptions. They start to wonder, "If they can do it, why can't I?" They start to recognize that the voice saying "That's not for us" was never their own voice, it was an echo of an era that no longer exists.

This is why personal transformation is not personal at all. It is communal. It is generational. Every time we challenge a limiting belief, we loosen its grip on the entire culture. Every time we claim a new experience, we widen the path for those who follow. Every time we break through a barrier, we weaken the illusion that the barrier ever belonged there.

The truth is, the "That's what white people do" mentality is not dying because we are pushing it aside. It is dying because we are outgrowing it. We are stepping into a new understanding of who we are and what we deserve. We are realizing that the world is far bigger than the version presented to us in childhood. And we are recognizing that our souls have always been calling us toward expansion, even when the world told us to shrink.

The future will not be defined by the limits we inherited. It will be defined by the possibilities we choose to embrace. And as more and more Black people awaken to the truth of their own boundless potential, we will continue to dismantle not just external barriers, but internal ones. We will continue to step into a world that reflects the fullness of our humanity. And we will continue to prove, in quiet and powerful ways, that there is nothing, absolutely nothing, we cannot do.

"If you know whence you came, there is really no limit to where you can go."

— **James Baldwin**

CHAPTER 3

BUT WHAT ABOUT SLAVERY?

Honoring the Past, Healing Its Residue, and Refusing to Be Defined by It

Whenever I share my belief that the future of Black America is brighter than ever, there's one question that almost always arises, sometimes spoken with genuine curiosity, sometimes with disbelief, and sometimes with anger wrapped in pain: *"But what about slavery?"* It is a question shaped by history, memory, trauma, and the undeniable truth that the wounds of the past still echo in the present. To talk about the progress we've made without honoring where we began would be irresponsible. To speak of optimism without acknowledging the depth of the suffering our ancestors endured would be disrespectful.

So, let's talk about slavery. Let's talk about what it was, what it left behind, and why, despite its lingering shadows, it cannot define our future unless we allow it to.

There is no denying that slavery was one of the most dehumanizing systems ever constructed on this planet. It wasn't only physical bondage; it was psychological warfare designed to strip a people of their identity, sever cultural memory, and crush the human spirit. It sought to break the body, distort the mind, and annihilate the soul. Yet even under the weight of such brutality, Black people produced love, community, music, spirituality, ingenuity, resistance, and hope. That alone tells us something profound: slavery did not destroy us. It tried. But it failed.

And the fact that it failed is the beginning of the story of our optimism.

What often goes unspoken is how extraordinary it is that a people subjected to such sustained brutality did not internalize hatred as their defining posture. That outcome was far from guaranteed. History is filled with examples of groups who endured trauma and emerged fractured, consumed by vengeance or despair. Yet again and again, Black communities chose connection over collapse.

This choice was not accidental. It reflected a deep, intuitive understanding of something essential about human survival. Hatred corrodes the vessel that carries it. Joy, even when fragile, sustains life. Faith, even when tested, creates continuity. And meaning, even when difficult to articulate, gives suffering a direction rather than an endpoint.

This is why spirituality, music, humor, and storytelling were not luxuries during slavery. They were technologies of survival. They were ways of preserving identity when every external force attempted to erase it. The presence of joy under such conditions was not denial. It was defiance.

That same defiant joy still pulses through Black culture today. It is not evidence of forgetting. It is evidence of remembering who we are beneath the trauma.

THE LINGERING SHADOWS OF AN OLD SYSTEM

To say "slavery is in the past" is both true and incomplete. Slavery as an institution ended generations ago, but its psychological residue still lives in the collective consciousness of America. It shows up in subtle ways: in unconscious biases, in internalized inferiority, in distorted narratives about Black intelligence and ability, in systemic disparities that trace their roots back to a time when Black humanity was not recognized by law.

Ignoring these remnants doesn't make them disappear. Acknowledging them doesn't make us weak. In fact, acknowledging them makes us strong. It gives us clarity. It helps us understand why certain patterns exist so we can finally break them. The trauma of slavery didn't vanish simply because the chains were removed; the trauma passed from generation to generation through stories, through silence, through fear, through survival strategies designed for a world far harsher than the one we live in today.

Many of the beliefs we carry as a community, beliefs about danger, about trust, about opportunity, about identity, can be traced back to the emotional DNA of people trying to stay alive in a system that was trying to erase them. These beliefs weren't born from weakness. They were born from brilliance. They were mental strategies that kept people alive. But strategies that once ensured survival can become barriers when the world around us changes.

And this is the heart of the matter:
The world *has* changed.
The consciousness of humanity *has* evolved.
And we are no longer living in the conditions that created those strategies.

Generational trauma is often misunderstood as something mystical or abstract. In reality, it is deeply practical. Trauma shapes behavior, and behavior shapes culture. When people are forced to live under constant threat, vigilance becomes a virtue. When trust is dangerous, skepticism becomes wisdom. When safety is uncertain, control becomes necessary.

These adaptations made sense in a world where freedom was fragile and consequences were lethal. But when the environment changes, adaptations that once protected can begin to constrain. What once kept people alive can quietly limit how fully they live.

Recognizing this does not invalidate the past. It contextualizes it.

The question then becomes not "Why do these patterns exist?" but "Are these patterns still needed?" And asking that question is not an act of betrayal. It is an act of evolution.

Evolution honors what came before by building upon it, not by freezing it in place.

THE POWER AND DANGER OF HISTORICAL MEMORY

History is a teacher, but it can also be a prison if we don't know how to carry it. Too many people mistake remembering the past with reliving it. Too many believe that honoring our ancestors requires identifying with their suffering. But suffering was not their identity; survival was. Resilience was. Faith was. Creativity was. Joy was. Family was. And possibility — even in the darkest hours, was.

Our ancestors were never meant to be symbols of our limitations. They were meant to be symbols of our power.

When we say, "But what about slavery?" as a rebuttal to optimism, we unintentionally reinforce the idea that slavery is still controlling our destiny. We give power to an institution that no longer exists. We bind ourselves to ghosts. We become loyal to a narrative that keeps us small.

But liberation requires us to distinguish between history and identity.

History is what happened to us.
Identity is who we choose to become.

Slavery may explain where we started, but it cannot determine where we're going, not unless we keep telling ourselves that the past holds more authority over our future than our present consciousness does.

There is also a psychological phenomenon worth naming here. When a community continually tells its story primarily through the lens of suffering, that story can unintentionally become a ceiling rather than a foundation. It defines identity by what was endured instead of what was expressed through endurance.

This is not unique to Black America. It is a human pattern. Nations, families, and individuals can all become tethered to formative trauma if reflection is not paired with integration. Healing requires both remembrance and release.

Release does not mean forgetting. It means no longer allowing the memory to dictate the present.

The most powerful way to honor ancestors is not to replicate their pain, but to live the freedom they were denied. Their struggle was not meant to be inherited as burden. It was meant to be inherited as possibility.

AMERICA IS NOT WHAT IT WAS — AND NEITHER ARE WE

There is a tendency, especially in younger generations, to believe that nothing has changed because injustice still exists. But progress does not mean perfection; progress means evolution. And evolution is exactly what has happened.

Black Americans today exist in a different psychological, social, and spiritual landscape than our ancestors. We have access to resources, knowledge, education, technology, and opportunity that would have been unimaginable even 60 years ago. A Black billionaire was once a fantasy; now we have several. A Black president was once unthinkable; now it's part of American history. Black doctors, entrepreneurs, scholars, creators, innovators, and leaders exist at a scale our ancestors could barely dream of.

This is not accidental.
This is evolution.
This is consciousness rising.
This is the unfolding of human possibility.

The remnants of slavery still exist, but they are cracks, not walls. We walk through doors today that were sealed shut for centuries. And each generation pushes those doors open wider. Our grandparents fought to survive. Our parents fought to be recognized. Our generation fights to be free in ways they never even had the privilege to imagine.

We are not the same people we were 100 years ago.
We are not even the same people we were 30 years ago.
And the world is not the same world it was.

Another often overlooked truth is that progress does not always announce itself in ways that feel emotionally satisfying. It rarely arrives all at once, and it rarely aligns perfectly with our expectations. Progress tends to be uneven, contradictory, and frustratingly incomplete.

But it is still progress.

When we focus exclusively on what remains broken, we can miss what is actively being built. We can overlook the fact that Black Americans today participate in shaping global culture, influencing politics, driving innovation, and redefining success at unprecedented levels.

This does not mean injustice has ended. It means injustice no longer has a monopoly on the narrative.

The presence of struggle does not negate the presence of growth. Both can exist simultaneously. And recognizing growth does not require minimizing pain. It requires expanding perspective.

WHY SLAVERY CANNOT BE THE CENTER OF OUR IDENTITY

There is a subtle danger in over-identifying with historical trauma: it keeps us reactive instead of proactive. When slavery becomes the central story of Black identity, it steals energy that could be used for creation, innovation, healing, and progress. It keeps the wound open instead of allowing the scar to form.

A scar is not a sign of defeat. It is a sign of healing.

When we carry slavery as a scar, a reminder of what we survived, it becomes a source of pride and strength. But when we carry slavery as an open wound, it becomes a limitation that shapes our beliefs about what is possible.

Identity should be rooted in power, not pain.
In possibility, not oppression.
In creation, not constraint.

This is not denial.
This is evolution.

We honor our ancestors not by clinging to their suffering, but by expanding beyond it.

Centering identity around possibility does something subtle but profound. It changes the questions we ask. Instead of asking, "Why does this keep happening to us?" we begin asking, "What do we want to create next?" Instead of measuring ourselves against historical limitations, we begin measuring ourselves against emerging potential.

This shift does not erase accountability for injustice. It simply refuses to let injustice monopolize imagination.

Imagination is a form of power. It shapes policy, culture, and personal decision-making long before outcomes appear in the world. When imagination is constrained by the past, the future contracts. When imagination is liberated, possibilities multiply.

This is why optimism is not a feeling. It is a strategy.

THE REAL LEGACY OF SLAVERY IS NOT TRAUMA — IT IS TRIUMPH

The fact that Black Americans are still here is a miracle. A miracle of resilience. A miracle of spirit. A miracle of human determination.

The real legacy of slavery is not the brutality we endured, it is the brilliance we preserved.

It is our capacity to love despite trauma.
To build despite destruction.
To laugh despite sorrow.
To hope despite evidence.
To dream despite danger.
To rise despite resistance.

We did not inherit brokenness.
We inherited brilliance.
We inherited strength.
We inherited the blueprint for survival.
And now we have the opportunity to turn survival into ascendence.

This is why slavery, though tragic, though horrific, though foundational to America's early economic system, cannot be the center of our future narrative.

Our power is too great.
Our genius too undeniable.
Our potential too expansive.

There is also a generational dimension to this moment that deserves recognition. Younger generations are not rejecting history. They are renegotiating their relationship with it. They are asking how to honor the past without being consumed by it. How to remember without remaining tethered. How to respect ancestors while choosing a different emotional inheritance.

This is not amnesia. It is discernment.

They are intuitively sensing that the future requires a different posture than perpetual defense. That creativity, collaboration, and curiosity are more effective tools for expansion than constant resistance alone. And they are acting accordingly.

This generational shift is one of the clearest signs that consciousness is evolving.

CLOSING: THE COURAGE TO LOOK FORWARD

When people ask, "But what about slavery?" they are really asking, "How can we move forward with so much pain behind us?" And the answer is this:

We move forward the same way our ancestors did, by choosing to. By believing in a future they couldn't see. By trusting that the human spirit is stronger than any system designed to destroy it. By recognizing that what we overcame is evidence of what we are capable of becoming.

Slavery was a chapter, not the whole book.
It was a storm, not the climate.
It was a wound, not our identity.

And while we honor it, acknowledge it, and learn from it, we must never worship it.
We must never let it become the lens through which we see ourselves.
We must never allow it to dictate the scope of our dreams.

The future belongs to those who understand the past but refuse to be defined by it.

We have carried the weight of slavery long enough.
Now it is time to carry the promise of our potential.

Yet even as we step into this new understanding, it's important to acknowledge that healing is not a linear journey. It doesn't happen all at once, and it doesn't look the same for everyone. Some people need space to grieve. Some need to learn. Some need to forgive. Some need to reclaim what was taken. And some simply need to be reminded that it is okay to move forward without carrying the entire weight of our history on their shoulders.

Healing from something as vast and generational as slavery requires compassion, not just for our ancestors, but for ourselves. It requires us to recognize that the patterns we see in our communities didn't emerge from nowhere. They came from centuries of intentional disruption, displacement, and psychological conditioning. And when we understand that, we begin to treat ourselves and our people with a kind of tenderness that has been missing for far too long.

But compassion is only one side of healing. The other side is courage. The courage to rewrite the story. The courage to imagine ourselves outside of the narratives we inherited. The courage to dream in a world that once tried to make dreaming illegal. The courage to trust our evolution, even when parts of us still feel connected to the pain of the past.

And that courage is rising. I see it everywhere. I see it in young Black activists who refuse to let old systems shape their identity. I see it in Black entrepreneurs building companies their great-grandparents could never have fathomed. I see it in families reclaiming emotional wellness, prioritizing mental health, and breaking generational patterns. I see it in artists, writers, filmmakers, and creators boldly telling stories from our perspective, stories filled not just with trauma, but with joy, intimacy, creativity, and possibility.

We are healing not by erasing our past, but by expanding beyond the limits that past imposed.

And perhaps the most powerful part of this moment is that we are no longer healing alone. We are healing collectively. We are healing publicly. We are healing with tools and language our ancestors never had access to: trauma-informed therapy, spiritual awakening, generational psychology, ancestral reconnection, mindfulness, meditation, journaling, and a global community of Black voices who are all committed to rising together.

The scars of slavery will never fully disappear, nor should they. They remind us of what we survived. But scars should not control movement; they should simply remind us of our strength. They mark where the wound once was, not where the wound still is.

And this is why optimism about our future is not naïve, it is inevitable. Because any people who can endure what we endured, and still produce brilliance, still create beauty, still build families, still raise leaders, still shape global culture, and still rise generation after generation… that is a people whose destiny is expansion.

The question is no longer whether the remnants of slavery exist. They do. The more important question is whether those remnants have the power to define our future.

And the answer is no. Not anymore.

We stand on the shoulders of giants, but we are not bound by their battles. We honor their fight, but we are not required to relive it. We carry their strength, but we are free to pursue a life they only dreamed of. The future is not calling us to repeat the past, it is calling us to transcend it.

This is the moment when we step into a new understanding of ourselves.
A new sense of what is possible.
A new identity rooted in power, purpose, and awakening.

And when we embrace that truth, slavery becomes not an anchor, but a reference point, a reminder of how far we've come and how far we are destined to go.

The past shaped us.
But the future?
The future belongs to us.

At some point, every people must decide whether history will serve as a compass or a cage. A compass helps orient direction. A cage restricts movement. The difference lies not in the past itself, but in how the past is held.

When slavery is understood as something we overcame rather than something that defines us, it becomes a source of wisdom rather than weight. It sharpens discernment without dulling hope. It strengthens resolve without constricting imagination.

And that is where true healing lives.

Not in denial.
Not in obsession.
But in integration.

We integrate the past, then we transcend it. We carry forward what strengthens us and release what no longer serves growth. That is how individuals mature. That is how cultures evolve. And that is how a people step fully into their future.

"Joy is not ignorance of the struggle.
It is the evidence that the struggle did not
get the final word."

— **Michael Taylor**

THE TRIALS AND TRIUMPHS OF A JOYFUL BLACK MAN IN AMERICA

A Personal Reflection by Coach Michael Taylor

Before we move into the reasons for optimism and the rise of a new Black consciousness, I want to share something deeply personal. The previous chapters explored collective history, slavery, stereotypes, limiting beliefs, and the psychology of a people navigating an oppressive system. But history does not live only in textbooks or timelines. It lives in the bodies, minds, and hearts of individuals.

And if I am going to illuminate the path forward, then it is only right that I share my own journey through the shadows and into the light. This reflection is not an intellectual argument. It is not theory. It is the story of how I confronted the lingering effects of racism, internalized pain, and generational wounds, and how I ultimately discovered joy, freedom, and a deeper spiritual truth.

I offer it here as a bridge between our past and our future, between pain and possibility, between what we were given and what we choose to create.

~~~

Growing up as a young black male in the inner-city projects of Corpus Christi Texas I was acutely aware that being "black" somehow made me different. As I watched television and looked through magazines and books I realized that the people I perceived to have all of the wealth were white people. When I asked my mom the reason for this her response was that there were lots of blacks that were wealthy,
~~~

but the white people did not want to show that on television. When asked why not, she responded by saying that this was the way that white people could control the minds of black people and keep them from attaining wealth. Even as a child, there was something about that comment that I did not agree with. I wanted to understand how the mind worked and most of all I wanted to understand how white people could control the minds of black people?

As I progressed through elementary school I remember the tension and fear I felt as I interacted with white kids in my class. At the age of nine I had my first experience of racism when a white female classmate approached me after a spelling test. In this class the person who scored an A on a test would receive a gold star, which was then placed on a poster board in plain view for all the students to see. It just so happened that I had the most gold stars of anyone in the class and the teacher would always encourage me to do well and to be comfortable being at the top of the class intellectually and academically. After this particular test the white female classmate came up to me and said, "my mom says that all niggers are dumb and stupid and even though you may have more stars than I do I am still smarter than you". I stood there in shock and disbelief and was unable to respond. Even though I had the evidence to refute her comments, as a nine-year-old the pain of her words cut me like a knife. I felt angry yet ashamed because this was not the first time I had heard those words. But this was the first time that I had heard them targeted directly at me by one of my peers.

My most painful experience of blatant racism occurred when I was seventeen. I was in high school and I met and fell in love with my high school sweetheart. She was a wonderful supportive caring person that incidentally happened to be white. When we met, she was somewhat of a wild child. She came from a pretty wealthy family yet hated her father and was into drugs cond rebellion. She was a C and D student that liked to skip school and hang out at the beach with her friends. After going out with her for a while I convinced her to turn her life around and give up the skipping school and abusing drugs.

She changed her attitude and became an A and B student. We were extremely close and shared that high school infatuated kind of love that feels so deep that it stays with you for a lifetime. After going out with her for over a year her father found out that we were dating. One night I got a phone call from him and it was obvious that he was not happy.

As he began speaking, I knew that I needed to keep my cool and not disrespect him. I listened to his objections and gave him an opportunity to get everything off of his chest. When he finished, I made the mistake of telling him that he did not have the right to decide whom his daughter should date. I tried to convince him that I had been a good influence on his daughter and that he should be happy that she was doing so well. My hope was that I could get him to understand that I was a good guy that was actually good for his daughter. Of course he could not hear a word I was saying. He was adamant about the fact that he knew what was best for his daughter and I was just some young punk trying to take advantage of his little girl. After screaming his disapproval of our relationship for several minutes he then said something that completely caught me off guard. Although I knew he was angry I did not expect to hear these words, "There is no way that I will allow my daughter to date a nigger. I will kill you before I let that happen". Although the words were painful, it was the venomous feeling of anger and hatred that came through the phone that ripped out my heart. Even today almost thirty years later I can still feel the hatred in his words. His anger came from deep within his soul and it was apparent that his anger wasn't just about me but about all black people.

As I sat there in disbelief, I immediately went numb. A part of me wanted to defend myself and curse at him and retaliate in some way. My initial feeling was anger, which I quickly subdued to avoid getting into a shouting match. Another part of me was extremely afraid because I did not know whether or not he would actually attempt to take my life. But the feeling I remember most after his comment was sadness. I remember a sinking feeling in my gut that was the result of being invalidated as a human being. I knew that he viewed me as less than a man and in his mind I was not good enough for his daughter simply because I was black. It was dehumanizing and demoralizing. How could this man hate me so much and not know anything about me? How could he pass judgment on me without ever seeing me or speaking to me? Why could he not see the positive influence I had had on his daughter? Why was I not allowed the opportunity to meet with him and talk to him so that he could see how much I really cared about his daughter and that my intentions were to simply love and support her?

So many questions so few answers.

I share these three true personal stories because as a black man I realize that my experiences are really just a microcosm of the challenges facing black men even today. I personally believe that our media still does an irresponsible job of portraying black people in general. The media generated perception is that being black is synonymous with being poor, uneducated, unmotivated and somehow a burden on society. Although I do not believe that the media can control how black people think, I am aware of the power that the media does have on a person's perception. Since a person's perception is their reality, the media definitely has an influence on people's minds.

It is my fervent belief that people in general are not born racist. Hatred is not a part of a person's genetic makeup. Racism is something that is learned and people usually learn from the environments in which they are raised. Unfortunately, there are still some parents that teach their children that black people are inferior as human beings and sadly enough some black people have accepted this as true.

As a black man, I realize that people are going to judge me and have preconceived ideas about who I am. I understand that no matter what I do the stereotypes of black men will precede me and somehow I will have to prove myself over and over again. I know that people will be afraid of me, will think less of me and put the label of "black" man on me no matter what I do.

So as a black man what can I do? How do I deal with the multiplicity of challenges that I face on a daily basis? Do I throw my hands up in defeat and give up? Do I accept the stereotypes and become just another black male statistic thrown into the ever-increasing prison population? Do I succumb to the pressure and lose my identity and try to become someone that I'm not?

In order for me to deal with the aforementioned challenges, I choose to first and foremost see myself as a man, not just a black man. If I see the world only through the lens of a black man I limit my perception of the world. When I let go of my attachment to being black first, I open the door to infinite possibilities for myself as a human being. This is not a denial of my ethnicity it is simply an affirmation of my true potential and my humanity. This awareness gives me an entirely new perspective on the world.

With this perspective I can honestly say that I absolutely love being a black man. I have come to this conclusion as a result of the past fifteen years of doing my emotional work and removing my shadows. I am now completely comfortable with who I am as a human being and I recognize that I am a man who happens to be black. I am proud of my racial heritage but the true source of my power transcends the color of my skin.

When I view the world from this perspective, I begin to recognize that although there is ignorance and hatred in the world, racism in and of itself is actually an over-used word in our society that keeps us separate and in denial of our oneness. This does not excuse injustice and oppression for people of color it simply acknowledges that racism is a disease of the mind. In objective scientific terms it isn't real. It is a manmade creation that exists only in our minds.

As I reflect over my personal mission statement: "As a man amongst men, I create a world of Love and understanding by loving myself and understanding others."

I fully grasp the implications of what these words mean to me. By loving myself and removing any blocks to my awareness, I am able to understand others without judgment. This allows me to constantly be in the moment without being attached to things that have happened to me in the past. By healing my anger and forgiving those who have hurt me I can be fully present to people in my life. Therefore, I do not think in over generalized statements and use words and phrases like those white people, or them and they. I live in the moment and address each individual situation in the moment. This is the beauty of healing your heart. It frees you from your past and keeps you in the present moment.

My intention is for you to have a new perception about black men after reading this article. The truth is we are no different than any other group of men. We are loving, caring, compassionate, sensitive, intelligent, forgiving and courageous. We love our country and our families. We deal with all of the same emotions and challenges as anyone else. We do not all blame society for our challenges and we are constantly making positive contributions to America. We are definitely an asset to this country not a liability.

I am reminded of a lesson I learned from Wayne Dyer in which he taught me that I should never focus my attention on that which I am against. Instead, I must focus my attention on that which I am for and I will experience that as a result. So instead of being against racism I am for unity. Instead of taking a position against hatred I take a stand for love.

As Dr. Martin Luther King Jr. said. "We're afraid of each other because we do not know one another, we do not know one another because most of us are separated from each other." My intention is to remove the perceived separation and create oneness. This is the driving force in my life. I want to be the change I want to see in the world and I invite you to join me in creating a world of love, peace and unity.

In the immortal words of John Lennon, "You may say that I'm a dreamer, but I'm not the only one. I hope someday you'll join us, and the world will be as one.'

Won't you join me?

CLOSING REFLECTION

As you've just read, my journey has included both trials and triumphs. I have felt the sting of racism, the ache of rejection, the weight of history, and the deep wounds that so many of us carry. But I have also discovered joy, not a joy that ignores suffering, but a joy that *transcends* it. A joy born from healing, awakening, and remembering who I really am beneath the scars.

This is why I can say with absolute certainty that our future is bright. Because if one man can rise above centuries of conditioning, false narratives, and internalized limitations, then so can a community. So can a generation. So can a people. My story is not an exception; it is a reflection of what becomes possible when consciousness expands.

And that's why the next chapter is so important. What you're about to read is not just a social trend or cultural shift, it is the awakening of a new Black identity rooted in power, possibility, and profound self-awareness.

Let us continue our journey forward…

"Know whence you came. If you know whence
you came, there is really no limit
to where you can go."

— **James Baldwin**

INTERLUDE II

BUT WHAT ABOUT BLACK MEN?

Few figures in American culture have been more misunderstood, misrepresented, or mythologized than the Black man. Long before many Black boys understand who they are, they are taught who the world believes them to be. These beliefs do not emerge organically. They are manufactured, repeated, and reinforced through media, policy, entertainment, and collective imagination.

The Black man has been framed as a problem to be managed rather than a human being to be understood.

This distortion did not begin with individual prejudice. It emerged from the same inherited belief system that shaped slavery, segregation, and structural inequality. Over time, that system learned to survive by reshaping itself. Chains were replaced with narratives. Control was replaced with caricature. Fear became the most efficient tool of all.

Media portrayals narrowed Black masculinity into a handful of tropes: violent, absent, hypersexual, emotionally unavailable, dangerous. These images were repeated so often that they began to feel normal, even inevitable. And what is repeated long enough begins to feel true, not only to those who consume the images, but to those who are forced to live inside them.

This is the cruelest trick of the inherited belief system: it does not simply impose limitations from the outside. It invites them to be internalized.

To speak honestly about Black men, we must acknowledge real challenges without allowing those challenges to define identity. Yes, incarceration rates are disproportionately high. Yes, violence impacts too many communities. Yes, suicide and untreated mental health struggles among Black men are rising. These realities must be named, not avoided.

But they must also be **contextualized**.

They are not proof of deficiency. They are evidence of prolonged exposure to systems that punish vulnerability, criminalize survival, and deny emotional support while demanding strength. When boys are taught that expressing fear is weakness, that asking for help is failure, and that survival requires emotional armor, the cost eventually surfaces.

What has too often been framed as moral failure is more accurately understood as unmet humanity.

And yet, even within this context, something remarkable is happening.

Across the country and beyond, Black men are rejecting the scripts they were handed. They are questioning inherited definitions of masculinity. They are choosing healing over silence, purpose over performance, community over isolation. They are naming trauma without being consumed by it. They are redefining what strength looks like.

Movements focused on Black male empowerment are not emerging in response to despair. They are emerging in response to **awakening**.

Organizations, initiatives, and cultural platforms centered on Black men are shifting the narrative from pathology to possibility. They emphasize identity, leadership, emotional literacy, responsibility, and self-definition. They reject the lie that Black masculinity must be hardened to survive. They offer a new truth: that wholeness is not weakness, and joy is not denial.

This shift matters not only for Black men, but for families, communities, and future generations. When Black men are seen fully, they lead differently. They parent differently. They love differently. They build differently. And the ripple effects extend far beyond individual lives.

The future does not belong to a people trapped inside distorted mirrors. It belongs to those who reclaim the authority to define themselves.

Black men are doing that work now. Quietly. Publicly. Imperfectly. Courageously.

And that reclamation is not a side note to the future.
It is central to it.

"Caring for myself is not self-indulgence,
it is self-preservation."

— **Audre Lorde**

BUT WHAT ABOUT BLACK WOMEN?

If Black men have been misrepresented in American culture, Black women have been overburdened by it. They have been asked to carry strength without rest, leadership without recognition, and resilience without relief. They have been celebrated for endurance while being denied protection, support, and softness.

From the earliest chapters of American history, Black women were forced into roles that demanded everything while offering little in return. They labored physically, emotionally, and spiritually, often at the center of families and communities that depended on their steadiness for survival. Over time, this necessity hardened into expectation.

Strength became assumed.
Sacrifice became normalized.
Exhaustion became invisible.

The image of the "strong Black woman" was born not as a compliment, but as a coping mechanism in a society that refused to see Black women as fully human. What began as resilience in the face of injustice gradually transformed into a standard that left little room for vulnerability.

This, too, is a distortion of the inherited belief system.

Black women have been praised for being unbreakable while rarely being asked what it costs to remain so. They have been admired for perseverance while being denied the conditions that make rest, care, and ease possible. Invisibility has often accompanied visibility, and recognition has come without protection.

To speak honestly about Black women, we must acknowledge this duality.

Black women have faced disproportionate economic challenges, health disparities, and emotional labor both inside and outside their communities. They are often expected to lead, nurture, advocate, and endure simultaneously. The weight of these expectations is real, and the toll it takes is profound.

Yet this reality does not tell the full story.

What is too often overlooked is that Black women have not merely survived these conditions. They have shaped culture, driven movements, built institutions, and expanded the boundaries of what leadership looks like. They have done so not by abandoning their humanity, but by insisting on it, even when the world resisted.

Across generations, Black women have been at the forefront of social change, economic innovation, artistic expression, and community building. They have organized when systems failed. They have created when resources were scarce. They have led with clarity, courage, and care, often without acknowledgment.

Their influence is woven into every aspect of American life and increasingly recognized on a global stage.

What is changing now is not the presence of Black women's power, but the **visibility and valuation** of it. The cultural narrative is beginning to catch up with reality. Black women are no longer confined to supporting roles or symbolic leadership. They are recognized as architects of ideas, movements, and futures.

This shift matters deeply.

As Black women reclaim the right to define themselves beyond endurance, they are redefining success, leadership, and care. They are challenging the belief that worth is measured by how much one can carry without breaking. They are choosing wholeness over heroism, balance over burnout, and joy over obligation.

This is not a retreat from strength.
It is a refinement of it.

A new generation of Black women is growing up with expanded possibilities. They see themselves reflected as entrepreneurs, scholars, artists, innovators, healers, and leaders across every field. They are exposed to narratives that affirm complexity rather than confinement. They are learning that ambition does not require self-erasure and that care is not weakness.

This cultural shift has ripple effects far beyond individual lives. When Black women are supported, families stabilize. When they are valued, communities thrive. When their leadership is recognized, systems change.

The future does not ask Black women to save it through sacrifice. It invites them to shape it through vision.

And perhaps most importantly, Black women are increasingly giving themselves permission to exist beyond expectation. They are setting boundaries. They are prioritizing mental, emotional, and physical health. They are redefining success on their own terms.

This self-definition is revolutionary.

Because when Black women no longer measure themselves by inherited standards of strength, they unlock new forms of power rooted in clarity, creativity, and connection. They model a future where leadership includes rest, where excellence includes care, and where contribution does not require depletion.

The future belongs to those who are whole.

Black women are claiming that wholeness now, not as an act of defiance, but as an act of truth. They are stepping into a future that honors their humanity as much as their contribution.

And that shift, quiet and profound, is not a footnote in the story of what comes next.

It is one of its driving forces.

"Black consciousness is the realization by the
Black man of the need to rally together…
around the cause of their oppression."

— **Steve Biko**

CHAPTER 4

REASON #1: THE RISE OF A NEW BLACK CONSCIOUSNESS

Awakening, Healing, and the Evolution of Our Identity

There is a quiet revolution happening in Black America — not the kind that makes headlines, not the kind that politicians argue about on television, not the kind that institutions rush to define. It is a revolution taking place in the minds and hearts of everyday people who are waking up to the truth of who they really are. A revolution rooted in awareness, healing, inner transformation, and a refusal to be confined by the narratives handed down through history.

For generations, Black identity in America was shaped by the shadows of oppression. We were portrayed through the lens of deficit, struggle, danger, or survival. Even when we weren't consciously absorbing those narratives, they subtly shaped how we saw ourselves and how the world responded to us. But today, something profoundly different is happening. We are no longer defining ourselves through the lens of what we escaped. We are defining ourselves through the lens of what we are becoming.

This is the rise of a new Black consciousness — a consciousness not rooted in trauma, but rooted in truth. Not shaped by pain, but shaped by possibility. Not limited by the past, but liberated by the future.

And this shift is not a trend. It is an evolution.

What makes this moment distinct from previous periods of cultural awakening is that this consciousness is not emerging in opposition to something. It is not fueled primarily by protest or resistance, although both still matter. Instead, it is emerging from a deeper internal recognition. A realization that identity does not have to be constructed in response to harm. It can be constructed in alignment with truth.

This distinction is subtle, but essential.

When identity is built in reaction, it remains tethered to the very forces it seeks to escape. When identity is built in alignment, it becomes self-sustaining. It no longer requires an enemy to define itself. It requires only clarity.

That is what is changing now.

More Black people are recognizing that their worth is inherent, not conditional. That their value does not depend on overcoming struggle, disproving stereotypes, or outperforming expectations. It exists prior to achievement. This recognition is quietly dismantling the internal pressure to constantly prove legitimacy.

And when the need to prove dissolves, freedom expands.

A CONSCIOUSNESS BEYOND THE OLD STORY

We are living in a time when Black people are asking deeper questions than ever before. Questions about purpose. Questions about identity. Questions about spirituality. Questions about healing. Questions about the narratives we inherited and whether they still serve us. We are not simply accepting what society says about us; we are examining it, challenging it, and replacing it with a truth that resonates with our soul instead of our fear.

This new consciousness is visible everywhere you look. It's in the rise of Black therapists, healers, meditation teachers, yoga instructors, trauma specialists, and spiritual leaders who are leading our community toward emotional and psychological liberation. It's in the growing number of Black people engaging in conversations about generational trauma, mindfulness, personal development, and mental health — subjects once considered taboo or "not for us."

But beyond that, it's in the sense of self returning to our community. A remembering. A reclaiming. A lifting of a veil that for so long obscured our greatness. People are waking up to the realization that they are not broken, damaged, inferior, or powerless. They are divine, creative, resilient, brilliant, and deeply capable of shaping their reality.

This is not just individual awakening — it is collective evolution.

Collective evolution does not happen because everyone agrees at once. It happens because enough people begin to operate from a new internal reference point. Over time, this new reference point becomes visible in behavior, language, priorities, and relationships.

We are seeing that now.

Conversations that once felt radical are becoming mainstream within our communities. Emotional intelligence is no longer dismissed as weakness. Boundaries are no longer interpreted as rejection. Therapy is no longer framed as something only needed in crisis. These shifts signal a maturing culture.

Maturity does not mean perfection. It means responsibility.

A mature consciousness recognizes that healing is ongoing, that growth requires patience, and that expansion involves discomfort. It understands that awakening does not eliminate struggle, but it does change how struggle is metabolized.

Instead of internalizing pain as identity, the new consciousness processes pain as information. It asks, "What is this here to teach?" rather than "What is wrong with me?"

That single shift changes everything.

WE ARE QUESTIONING THE SCRIPTS WE INHERITED

Part of the rise in Black consciousness is the growing willingness to question the scripts passed down from earlier generations. Scripts rooted in survival. Scripts rooted in caution. Scripts rooted in an America that no longer exists in the same form. Many of the beliefs that guided our grandparents and great-grandparents were formed in an era where the primary goal was survival, not self-actualization. Their world demanded alertness, caution, and emotional armor.

But our world — while still imperfect — offers possibilities they never had the privilege to imagine.

The new consciousness recognizes this shift. It says:

"I honor where I came from,
but I will not let yesterday's fear determine tomorrow's potential."

We are learning to distinguish between inherited beliefs that kept us alive and inherited beliefs that keep us limited. This is what consciousness does — it creates separation between what is true and what is simply familiar.

And once that separation exists, transformation becomes inevitable.

This discernment is one of the most sophisticated skills a culture can develop. It requires both gratitude and courage. Gratitude for the strategies that ensured survival, and courage to acknowledge when those strategies are no longer aligned with growth.

Survival-based beliefs often sound like wisdom. They are familiar. They feel protective. But familiarity does not always equal truth. And protection is not the same as expansion.

The new Black consciousness is not dismissing the past. It is contextualizing it. It is recognizing that strategies forged under extreme conditions were never meant to be permanent operating systems. They were bridges, not destinations.

When a people recognize that, they gain access to a new level of choice.

Choice over reflex.
Choice over repetition.
Choice over inherited limitation.

This is not rebellion against elders. It is fulfillment of their sacrifices.

THE LANGUAGE OF HEALING AND SELF-AWARENESS IS EXPANDING

For the first time in our history, Black America is embracing healing not as a luxury, but as a necessity. Therapy, coaching, meditation, breathwork, journaling, and emotional awareness are becoming part of our cultural vocabulary. We are learning the patterns of trauma, recognizing the residue of oppression, and understanding the psychological impacts of our historical experiences — not to stay stuck in them, but to free ourselves from them.

This alone is a revolution.

Because a healed mind thinks differently.
A healed heart chooses differently.
A healed identity dreams differently.

Healing creates space.
And in that space, the truth of who we are can finally breathe.

The old consciousness was shaped by pain.
The new consciousness is shaped by intention.

Space is an underappreciated concept in conversations about liberation. Without space, nothing new can enter. Trauma compresses space. It narrows perception, limits imagination, and keeps the nervous system in a constant state of readiness.

Healing expands space.

As that space opens, people begin to feel their lives rather than simply manage them. They become more present. More intentional. More discerning about where they place their energy. They begin to recognize that not every battle requires engagement and not every challenge requires self-sacrifice.

This spaciousness is allowing Black people to reconnect with joy as a legitimate state of being, not a temporary escape from hardship. Joy is being reclaimed as a birthright, not a reward.

And joy, when reclaimed, becomes a powerful stabilizing force. It anchors people in the present while opening them to possibility.

SPIRITUAL AWAKENING AND THE RECLAIMING OF INNER POWER

A major aspect of this new consciousness is spiritual. Not religious — spiritual. Black Americans are exploring their relationship with the Divine in ways that transcend traditional dogma. They are connecting with a spirituality that affirms their worth, honors their identity, and reconnects them to their intuition. People are leaving behind fear-based religious structures and embracing a spirituality rooted in love, personal empowerment, and self-knowledge.

This spiritual shift is not accidental.
It is a natural progression of a people evolving beyond survival mode.

When you stop living in fear, you begin seeking meaning.
When you stop bracing for attack, you begin looking inward.
When you stop questioning your worth, you start exploring your purpose.

This deeper spiritual connection is helping Black people see themselves as more than their bodies, more than their history, more than the stereotypes placed upon them. It is awakening the truth that we are expressions of Divine Intelligence living out a human experience — not the other way around.

This shift in identity alone is enough to transform the future.

Spiritual awakening often arrives after identity has been stripped down to its essentials. When external definitions fail, people turn inward. When inherited narratives collapse, intuition rises.

This is why spirituality is emerging now in such a personal and expansive form. It is not about replacing one dogma with another. It is about direct relationship. Relationship with self. Relationship with meaning. Relationship with something greater than circumstance.

This inward turn is restoring a sense of agency that was eroded by generations of external definition. People are no longer asking, "Who am I allowed to be?" They are asking, "Who am I becoming?"

That question carries creative power.

REIMAGINING BLACKNESS THROUGH THE LENS OF POSSIBILITY

For so long, Black identity was defined by what happened to us. But a new generation is defining Black identity by what is possible for us. Blackness is no longer perceived as a deficit — it is understood as a gift. A source of cultural power, spiritual depth, creative brilliance, and ancestral genius.

This reimagining is happening in business, art, media, fashion, wellness, education, entrepreneurship, and technology. Black people are no longer asking for permission to exist fully. We are taking up space in ways our ancestors could not. We are rewriting narratives. We are creating platforms. We are dismantling stereotypes simply by living authentically and expansively.

The most powerful part of this shift is that it is not being led by institutions — it is being led by individuals. Everyday people. People who are choosing to see themselves as creators of their destiny rather than victims of circumstance.

This is how cultures change.
Not from the top down, but from the inside out.

THE FUTURE IS BRIGHT BECAUSE OUR MINDS ARE OPENING

The reason this new consciousness is such an important foundation for optimism is simple:

When a people change the way they see themselves, the world eventually follows.

Everything begins in the mind.

Before we build new systems, we imagine them.
Before we change our circumstances, we change our beliefs.
Before we claim new possibilities, we must believe they belong to us.

The new Black consciousness is a declaration:
"I will not live small.
I will not shrink.
I will not carry limits that were never mine to carry.
I will not identify with wounds that did not begin with me.
I choose expansion.
I choose healing.
I choose myself."

This shift is already reshaping families, relationships, careers, communities, and futures.

When people awaken, everything they touch transforms.

As this new consciousness takes root, it is reshaping how success is defined. Achievement is no longer measured solely by status, income, or recognition. It is increasingly measured by alignment, fulfillment, and integrity.

People are choosing paths that reflect who they are rather than who they were told to become. They are prioritizing peace alongside progress. They are redefining ambition to include sustainability, wellness, and meaning.

This is not a retreat from excellence. It is a refinement of it.

Excellence that requires self-abandonment is no longer acceptable. Excellence that honors the whole self is becoming the new standard.

CLOSING: A NEW IDENTITY FOR A NEW ERA

The rise of a new Black consciousness is more than a trend — it is a signal that we are entering a new era. An era where we define ourselves through the fullness of our humanity rather than the shadows of our history. An era where we choose healing over trauma, possibility over limitation, and identity over stereotype. An era where the world no longer determines who we are; we determine that for ourselves.

This is why the future belongs to us.

Because once a people begin to think differently, they begin to live differently.
And once they begin to live differently, they begin to shape the world in ways that once seemed impossible.

We are not who we used to be.
We are not who they told us we were.
We are not confined to the stories of yesterday.

We are awakening.
We are evolving.
We are rising.

And this — this shift in consciousness — is only the beginning.

And yet, even as this awakening unfolds, it's important to acknowledge that consciousness does not expand in a straight line. It expands in waves. There are moments of clarity followed by moments of confusion. Moments of growth followed by moments of contraction. This is not a sign of failure — it is a sign of humanity. Awakening is not a destination; it is a lifelong unfolding. And as a community, we are now embracing the truth that growth is not only possible, but necessary.

What makes this moment so powerful is that we are no longer awakening in isolation. We are awakening together. We are having conversations that would have been unthinkable two decades ago — conversations about identity, spirituality, ancestry, emotional wellness, mental health, boundaries, energy, intuition, trauma, purpose, and personal freedom. We are giving ourselves permission to ask deeper questions, to sit with discomfort, to explore new ideas, and to break patterns that have kept us confined for far too long.

This openness to inner work is one of the greatest signs of our evolution. Previous generations didn't have the luxury of introspection. They were fighting for physical safety, civil rights, economic survival, and basic human dignity. They did not have the space to contemplate consciousness because the world didn't give them the room to breathe. But now, because of their sacrifices, we do have that room. And we are using it to reimagine the very essence of who we are.

That reimagining is touching every area of life. It's influencing the way we parent, the way we partner, the way we handle conflict, the way we choose careers, and the way we define success. You can feel it in young Black people who are choosing wellness over burnout, authenticity over conformity, entrepreneurship over stagnation, and joy over struggle. You can hear it in the language we use — words like alignment, vibration, healing, boundaries, manifestation, accountability, and intuition have become part of our cultural discourse. We are speaking the language of evolution.

And this shift is not just intellectual — it is energetic. You can sense it in the way Black people are reclaiming their right to rest, to feel safe, to dream, and to exist without armor. You can sense it in the way we are building communities rooted in love rather than fear. You can sense it in the way we are allowing ourselves to feel worthy, whole, deserving, and enough.

A people who once had their consciousness forcibly suppressed are now experiencing a spiritual renaissance. And once consciousness rises, it never goes back to sleep. It may stumble, it may wrestle, it may resist — but it does not return to its old state. That is the nature of awakening. And that is why this new consciousness is irreversible.

Black America is entering a chapter defined not by reaction, but by creation. Not by wounds, but by wisdom. Not by limits, but by expansion. And as more of us awaken to the truth of our divine potential, we create a magnetic field of possibility that future generations will inherit without question.

This is why the future belongs to us. Because a people who know who they are cannot be controlled, confined, or diminished. Consciousness is the ultimate freedom. And we are finally stepping into it with open eyes, open hearts, and an unshakeable belief that our best days are not behind us — they are just beginning.

"When an entire people begin to question a lie,
the lie loses its power."

— **Bell hooks**

CHAPTER 5

THE COLLAPSE OF THE CWBS

Why Each Generation Is More Aware, Empathetic, and United

One of the most extraordinary transformations happening in America today is something many people overlook, misunderstand, or underestimate: the gradual collapse of the Collective White Belief System — the CWBS. This is the system we explored in earlier chapters, the invisible inheritance of a society built on racial hierarchy, mythologies of superiority, and fabricated narratives about human worth. It shaped the psychology of this country for centuries. It justified the injustices. It sustained the stereotypes. It created the "us versus them" worldview that still lingers in certain pockets today.

But here is the most hopeful truth I can offer you:
The CWBS is dying.
Not quietly. Not gracefully. But undeniably.

It is collapsing under the weight of evolving consciousness, generational change, cultural exposure, increased diversity, global connection, and the simple but powerful act of human beings learning to see each other as human.

And the collapse of the CWBS is one of the strongest reasons to believe that Black America's future is brighter than our past.

What often makes the collapse of belief systems difficult to recognize is that they rarely disappear all at once. They erode unevenly. Some parts crumble quickly while others linger out of habit, fear, or nostalgia. This unevenness can create confusion, especially for those who expect progress to look clean or linear.

But belief systems do not dissolve through consensus. They dissolve through irrelevance.

When a worldview no longer explains reality, no longer organizes experience, and no longer produces results, it begins to lose its grip. People may still repeat its language, but they no longer live by its logic. They may defend it publicly, but privately they feel its emptiness.

This is where the CWBS now stands.

It still echoes in rhetoric, but it no longer commands allegiance in the way it once did. It feels outdated to younger generations, excessive to moderates, and emotionally exhausting even to those who attempt to defend it. What once felt like truth now feels like burden.

And belief systems that feel like burdens do not survive long.

THE INHERITANCE THAT NO LONGER FITS

The CWBS was never something white people consciously chose. It was something they inherited. It was the gravitational field of an old world — one built on fear, separation, domination, and control. It shaped how white Americans saw themselves and how they saw others. It was reinforced through family narratives, church pews, textbooks, movies, laws, and unspoken norms.

But something remarkable has happened in the past few decades.
The inheritance no longer fits.

Younger generations are questioning everything — their religion, their politics, their identity, their assumptions, and the stories they were taught about race. They are exposed to more diversity in one semester of school than many of their grandparents experienced in a lifetime. They engage with the world not through a narrow window of curated narratives, but through social media, global friendships, cultural exchanges, music, art, and conversations that transcend geography and identity.

The CWBS was constructed in isolation.
Isolation no longer exists.

This is the beginning of its collapse.

There is an important psychological dimension to inheritance that deserves attention here. Inherited beliefs are often accepted not because they are examined, but because rejecting them once carried social cost. Belonging required compliance. Questioning meant risk.

That risk has changed.

Younger generations are growing up in environments where questioning inherited narratives is not only tolerated, but encouraged. Critical thinking is normalized. Emotional literacy is valued. Diversity is experienced rather than theorized. As a result, allegiance to outdated belief systems feels less like loyalty and more like limitation.

This shift is subtle but powerful.

When people no longer fear social exile for questioning old ideas, those ideas lose their protection. They are exposed to scrutiny. And scrutiny is incompatible with illusion.

This is one of the quiet reasons the CWBS is collapsing. It no longer benefits from unquestioned loyalty.

EXPOSURE IS THE ANTIDOTE TO IGNORANCE

In the past, racial myths were sustained because people had little contact with anyone outside their group. Stereotypes go unchallenged when they exist in the absence of real relationships. But today, white Americans are dating Black partners, raising biracial children, attending multicultural schools, consuming Black music, Black culture, Black art, and Black thought at unprecedented levels.

You cannot fear what you have embraced.
You cannot dehumanize what you have learned from.
You cannot hate someone whose story you know.

Exposure melts stereotypes like sunlight dissolving shadows.

The CWBS cannot survive in a world where people experience daily evidence that contradicts everything it claims.

And that is exactly what's happening.

There is also something deeper happening beneath exposure itself. Exposure does not only challenge stereotypes. It expands emotional range. It allows people to feel empathy without effort, to experience resonance without instruction, and to relate without performance.

As emotional range expands, fear contracts.

Fear thrives in abstraction. It requires distance. It feeds on imagination ungrounded in reality. Exposure collapses that distance. It replaces imagined threats with real human presence. And once that presence is felt, fear loses coherence.

This is why connection is more transformative than confrontation.

When people form authentic relationships across difference, the CWBS does not need to be argued against. It becomes unnecessary. It fades quietly as something no longer needed to explain the world.

THE FRACTURE BETWEEN GENERATIONS

If you want clear proof of the CWBS collapsing, you only need to look at the widening gap between generations of white Americans.

The beliefs of an 80-year-old and the beliefs of a 20-year-old do not simply differ — they exist on different planets.

Younger generations are:

- More empathetic
- More culturally aware
- More educated about systemic injustice
- More relationally diverse
- More psychologically mature
- More comfortable challenging their own biases

They are not loyal to the old narratives.
They're not interested in preserving illusions.
They're not invested in defending superiority myths.

And this generational fracture is not small — it is seismic.

Every time an older worldview dies, a new possibility is born.
Every time a false belief dissolves, space is created for truth.

This is the quiet revolution that rarely makes the news.

But you can feel it everywhere.

Generational fracture is often framed as conflict, but it is more accurately understood as transition. Each generation inherits the unresolved tensions of the last and then decides, consciously or unconsciously, what to carry forward.

What is different now is the speed of transition.

Cultural evolution that once took centuries is now happening in decades. Information moves faster. Exposure is broader. Dialogue is constant. This accelerates consciousness in ways history has never seen before.

The result is not perfection, but momentum.

And momentum matters.

Momentum shifts norms. Norms shape institutions. Institutions shape lived experience. This is how belief systems collapse, not through dramatic overthrow, but through gradual displacement by something more functional.

THE CWBS CANNOT SURVIVE THE AGE OF CONSCIOUSNESS

We live in a time when people are exploring mindfulness, meditation, emotional intelligence, trauma healing, and spiritual awakening at unprecedented levels. This shift toward consciousness is incompatible with supremacist thinking. Supremacy requires fear. It requires separation. It requires illusion. Consciousness dissolves all three.

As people awaken to their own humanity, they naturally awaken to the humanity of others.

This is why racism feels increasingly out of place among awakened individuals — not because they have memorized social justice terminology, but because they have outgrown the emotional immaturity required to believe in racial hierarchy.

You cannot be spiritually awake and simultaneously believe that another human being is inferior.

The CWBS depends on unconsciousness.
Unconsciousness is dissolving.

Consciousness does not attack belief systems directly. It outgrows them. It renders them obsolete by offering a wider, more coherent understanding of reality. This is why awakening often feels like expansion rather than rebellion.

People who awaken do not need to be convinced that hierarchy is false. They feel it. They sense the incoherence of ranking human worth. They intuitively recognize that separation is artificial.

Once this recognition occurs, returning to supremacist thinking feels emotionally immature, not intellectually persuasive.

This is the quiet power of consciousness. It dissolves illusions by revealing their smallness.

THE INTERNET BROKE THE SPELL

Before the internet, people lived inside the narratives of their immediate environment. They believed what they were told. They accepted the identities assigned to them. The CWBS thrived in that containment.

But the internet shattered containment.

Now, white Americans can see:

- Black excellence
- Black innovation
- Black spirituality
- Black intelligence
- Black joy
- Black wisdom
- Black humanity

…in ways the old world tried desperately to hide.

When truth becomes visible, lies lose their power.

In a single scroll, a person can watch a Black astrophysicist explain the universe, a Black entrepreneur launch a startup, a Black father celebrating his children, a Black woman leading a meditation session, a Black filmmaker winning awards, a Black teenager going viral for brilliance or creativity.

The CWBS says one thing.
Reality now shows another.
And reality is winning.

Visibility has another important effect. It creates comparison. When people are exposed to a wide range of human expression, they begin to recognize excellence, creativity, and wisdom across boundaries that once felt rigid.

Comparison erodes myths.

When reality repeatedly contradicts inherited narratives, cognitive dissonance emerges. Over time, dissonance forces resolution. People either double down on illusion or release it. Increasingly, they are choosing release.

Not because they are pressured to, but because illusion is harder to sustain than truth.

WE ARE WITNESSING THE LOSS OF FEAR

At its root, racism is fear — fear projected outward and disguised as superiority. But fear is a fragile thing. It cannot survive exposure. It cannot survive truth. It cannot survive connection. It cannot survive in the presence of self-awareness.

When white Americans heal their own wounds — wounds of shame, guilt, identity confusion, insecurity, cultural loneliness — they become less likely to project those wounds onto others. The CWBS depended on unhealed people protecting their illusions. Healed people have no need for illusions.

As white Americans evolve emotionally, spiritually, and psychologically, they naturally detach from the belief systems that once shaped their ancestors.

This is not theoretical. It is observable.

As fear loosens its grip, something else emerges in its place: curiosity. Curiosity opens space for learning, humility, and self-reflection. It replaces defensiveness with inquiry.

Curiosity asks different questions.

Instead of "How do I protect what I have?" it asks "What can we build together?"
Instead of "Who is threatening me?" it asks "What am I afraid to face within myself?"

These questions lead to growth. Growth leads to integration. Integration leads to healing.

And healing leaves no room for supremacy.

BLACK AMERICA BENEFITS FROM THE COLLAPSE

Some people worry that acknowledging progress somehow diminishes the reality of racism. But acknowledging progress is not denial. It is empowerment.

The collapse of the CWBS means:

- Black children grow up in a world where more people see their brilliance.
- Black entrepreneurs face fewer psychological barriers.
- Black leaders are perceived with more legitimacy.
- Black art is celebrated rather than stolen or dismissed.
- Black love is normalized rather than fetishized or feared.
- Black identity expands rather than contracts.

As the CWBS weakens, Black potential strengthens.

This is one of the greatest reasons to be optimistic about the future.

THE COLLAPSE IS NOT QUIET — AND THAT'S GOOD

To the untrained eye, the increased visibility of racism looks like things are getting worse. But visibility is the *death rattle* of a dying system. Systems often scream loudest when their power is slipping away.

The anger, the backlash, the resistance — these are signs that the old identity is trying to hold on.

But collapse is irreversible.
A worldview born in 1619 cannot survive the consciousness of 2025.
It is dissolving.
And in its place, something new is emerging.

One of the most important implications of the CWBS collapsing is that it changes what is required of Black America. When the psychological infrastructure of oppression weakens, responsibility shifts. No longer are we defined primarily by resistance. We are increasingly defined by creation.

Creation requires a different posture.

It requires imagination. Vision. Strategy. Collaboration. And courage not only to confront injustice, but to build futures that were once inconceivable.

This is the moment we are entering now.

CLOSING: THE EVOLUTION OF A NATION

When you understand the CWBS not as a permanent cultural structure, but as a temporary belief system created by human minds, you realize something profound:

If humans created it, humans can outgrow it.

And that is exactly what is happening.

The CWBS is losing its grip.
A new understanding is rising.
A new America is forming.
A new consciousness is awakening.

And Black America stands ready to thrive in this new landscape —
not by waiting for permission,
but by stepping boldly into our potential
as the old illusions crumble behind us.

This is why the future belongs to us.
Because the beliefs that once tried to define us are dissolving,
and a new era — one rooted in truth, connection, and humanity — is
unfolding before our eyes.

And yet, even as we witness this collapse, we must recognize
something essential: belief systems do not disappear simply because
we intellectually reject them. They dissolve when enough people stop
feeding them. They crumble when the collective energy that once
sustained them is redirected toward something truer, healthier, and
more expansive. That is exactly what we are seeing across this country
— a massive redirection of psychological energy away from illusions
of superiority and toward the universal truth of shared humanity.

When you look closely, you can see the subtle ways this shift is showing
up. You see white parents teaching their children empathy instead of
avoidance. You see white teenagers openly rejecting the prejudices
of their elders. You see white educators confronting their biases and
reimagining how they teach history. You see white entrepreneurs
partnering with Black creators, not out of guilt or charity, but out of
genuine respect and admiration. You see interracial friendships and
relationships forming naturally, without the self-conscious weight
that once accompanied them. These are not small things. They are

signs of a collective awakening, signals that the old narrative is losing power.

What makes this moment truly remarkable is that the collapse of the CWBS is not solely the result of social pressure or political movements. It is the natural consequence of evolution. Human beings cannot awaken spiritually and remain loyal to beliefs rooted in separation. The two states are incompatible. Once you begin to see yourself as a conscious being — not a racial category, not a cultural identity, not a social construct — you begin to see others through the same expanded lens. Race becomes a descriptor, not a destiny. Identity becomes fluid, not fixed. Humanity becomes primary, not secondary.

And this is where hope becomes unavoidable. Because even though racism still exists — and will likely exist in some form as long as there are unhealed minds — the *foundation* that once supported it is eroding. The pillars are cracking. The psychological infrastructure is failing. And without that infrastructure, racism becomes an empty habit, a fragile echo of a world that no longer exists.

The old world is not dying because someone is killing it.
It is dying because the new world is more compelling.

It is dying because people — across races, generations, and backgrounds — are choosing connection over fear.
Curiosity over ignorance.
Compassion over projection.
Awareness over illusion.

The future is being shaped not by those who cling to the past, but by those who dare to imagine something better. And every time a white person chooses empathy over fear, every time they challenge the beliefs they inherited, every time they see a Black person not through the lens of stereotype but through the truth of shared humanity, another brick falls from the structure that once held us apart.

This is why the collapse of the CWBS is not something to fear — it is something to celebrate. It is evidence that consciousness is rising, that truth is replacing myth, that unity is replacing division, and that the future we dream of is already taking shape.

Black America does not have to wait for permission to rise.
We are rising because the world is finally evolving to meet our truth.
And as the old beliefs fade, our possibilities expand.

This is not the end of something.
It is the beginning.

"Definitions belong to the definers,
not the defined."

— **Toni Morrison**

CHAPTER 6

THE REBUILDING OF BLACK IDENTITY

From Trauma-Based Narratives to Possibility-Based Narratives

One of the most profound shifts happening in Black America today is the quiet, powerful rebuilding of our identity. For generations, Black identity was shaped through the lens of trauma. We inherited stories of struggle, survival, oppression, and resilience — and while these stories reflected truth, they also created a narrow psychological framework. They taught us how to endure but not always how to expand. They taught us how to navigate danger but not how to embrace possibility. They taught us how to protect ourselves but not always how to dream freely.

But today… something new is unfolding.

Black identity is being rewritten — not by institutions, not by media, not by systems of oppression, but by **Black people themselves.** We are reclaiming the narrative, reshaping the lens, and reconstructing the very definition of what it means to be Black in America. And what is emerging is nothing short of revolutionary.

For the first time in centuries, Black identity is shifting from trauma-based to possibility-based.
From reactive to creative.
From inherited to intentional.
From constrained to expansive.

This is one of the most powerful reasons to believe that the future belongs to us.

One of the reasons this shift feels so significant is that identity is not simply a personal construct. It is a social contract. It shapes how people treat us, how institutions respond to us, and how opportunities are extended or withheld. When a collective identity changes, the external world eventually recalibrates in response.

This is why internal shifts often precede external transformation.

When Black people begin to see themselves as expansive rather than constrained, the signals we send into the world change. Our posture changes. Our expectations change. Our boundaries change. We begin to move with a quieter confidence, one that does not require constant explanation or validation.

That confidence is contagious.

Others begin to respond differently, not because they have suddenly become enlightened, but because they are responding to a new energy, a new presence, a new way of being. Identity shapes interaction long before policy catches up.

WE WERE GIVEN A NARRATIVE — BUT WE ARE NO LONGER ACCEPTING IT

Every culture carries stories. But the stories Black Americans were given were not crafted for our empowerment. They were crafted to justify our oppression. Our identity was narrated by people who never understood us, valued us, or saw us clearly.

We were told we were inferior.
We were told we were dangerous.
We were told we were lazy.
We were told we were broken.
We were told we were victims of circumstance rather than creators of destiny.

Even the positive stories — the stories of strength and resilience — often defined us through what we survived rather than what we are capable of becoming.

But now, as consciousness evolves, we are questioning those stories. We are asking deeper questions:

Who told these stories?
Why did we believe them?
What stories are we choosing now?

And here is the truth:
The greatest revolution in Black America is not happening in politics, institutions, or public policy.
It is happening in the minds and hearts of Black people who are refusing to let anyone else define who they are.

Identity is power. When you reclaim your identity, you reclaim your life.
And that reclamation is happening everywhere.

Rejecting an imposed narrative does not happen all at once. It happens in moments. Moments where something feels off. Moments where an old explanation no longer fits lived experience. Moments where the gap between who we are and who we were told we are becomes impossible to ignore.

For many Black people, this awakening begins quietly. It may start with a book that reframes history, a conversation that challenges assumptions, or an experience that contradicts long held beliefs. At first, the mind resists. Familiar stories feel safer than unknown possibilities.

But once doubt enters, the story cannot be unseen.

From that point forward, identity reconstruction becomes inevitable. You may move slowly. You may hesitate. You may even retreat at times. But the old narrative no longer holds the same authority.

That is how transformation begins.

THE CULTURAL EXPANSION OF BLACK IDENTITY

Black identity was once confined to a handful of acceptable archetypes — the athlete, the entertainer, the activist, the survivor. Anything outside of that was often seen as "not Black enough" or "acting white." These limitations were not just external; they became internal, encoded into our psychology, shaping what we believed was possible for ourselves.

But today, the boundaries have exploded.

Black people are emerging as:

- Tech founders
- Meditation teachers
- Scientists
- Vegan chefs
- Environmental activists
- Yogis
- Philanthropists
- Global travelers
- Minimalists
- Astrophysicists
- Healers
- Spiritual guides
- Entrepreneurs
- Best-selling authors

Younger generations are redefining Blackness as fluid, multidimensional, curious, creative, spiritual, intellectual, adventurous, global, and whole.

The phrase "Black people don't do that" is fading from our vocabulary.
Because now?
Black people do *everything.*

This expansion alone is transformative because identity shapes destiny. When our identity is limited, our potential is limited. When our identity expands, our potential becomes limitless.

This expansion is doing more than adding new roles or professions to the image of Blackness. It is dissolving the idea that identity must be singular or fixed. Black identity is no longer something you fit into. It is something you express.

This shift allows people to stop choosing between parts of themselves.

You no longer have to choose between being intellectual and being Black. Spiritual and Black. Adventurous and Black. Soft and Black. Analytical and Black. There is room for complexity now.

Complexity is a sign of psychological health.

As this understanding spreads, younger generations are growing up without the same internal policing that constrained earlier ones. They are exploring identity as something fluid, creative, and self-directed. And that freedom is already producing new forms of leadership, artistry, and innovation.

MOVING BEYOND "STRUGGLE AS IDENTITY"

A subtle but powerful shift is happening: Black people are no longer defining themselves solely by what we've endured. Pain shaped us, but it does not define us. Trauma informed us, but it does not confine us.

For generations, "the struggle" was the backbone of Black identity — and for good reason. We survived the unimaginable. We built families, communities, art, spiritual traditions, music, storytelling, and culture under the worst conditions any human beings have ever faced. We earned every ounce of our pride.

But we are entering a new chapter.

In this chapter, identity is being built not on what we survived, but on who we are becoming.

We are shifting from:

- survival to creation
- pain to power
- protection to expansion
- reaction to intention
- trauma to transformation

Our identity is evolving from defensive to expressive.
From inherited to authored.
From reactive to visionary.

This shift opens possibilities we could never access while living inside a trauma-based identity.

Letting go of struggle as identity does not mean erasing struggle from memory. It means refusing to let struggle be the primary lens through which meaning is made. When pain becomes the organizing principle of identity, growth is unconsciously delayed.

Pain can teach, but it cannot lead.

Leadership requires vision. Vision requires imagination. And imagination requires space. This is why redefining identity away from constant struggle is not avoidance. It is preparation.

A future built from possibility requires people who can imagine beyond defense. Who can think beyond reaction. Who can move beyond survival mode and into creative mode.

That transition is happening now.

THE INFLUENCE OF HEALING WORK ON BLACK IDENTITY

One of the most beautiful things happening in our culture is the rise of emotional and spiritual healing among Black people. We are going to therapy. We are talking openly about mental health. We are learning about generational trauma. We are exploring meditation, journaling, self-reflection, and personal development. We are breaking family cycles that once seemed unbreakable.

Healing changes identity.

A healed Black person sees themselves differently:
Not as a threat.
Not as invisible.
Not as insufficient.
Not as oppressed.
Not as damaged.

But as worthy.
As whole.
As capable.
As divine.
As unlimited.

This is the foundation of a new identity — one grounded in self-love rather than self-protection.

Healing does more than soothe wounds. It restores authorship. When people heal, they stop seeing themselves as characters trapped in someone else's story. They begin to recognize themselves as narrators.

This shift is subtle but powerful.

A person who feels whole makes different choices. They tolerate less disrespect. They pursue opportunities aligned with their values.

They invest energy more wisely. They create from clarity rather than urgency.

As more Black people engage in healing work, identity becomes less reactive and more intentional. The self is no longer defined by what must be defended against, but by what deserves to be cultivated.

BLACK JOY AS A RADICAL ACT OF IDENTITY FORMATION

For generations, Black joy was seen as rebellion — a direct challenge to a society that expected us to remain broken. Today, Black joy is not just rebellion; it is identity. It is a declaration that our humanity is not defined by pain. It is proof that trauma cannot extinguish our light.

We see Black joy in:

- families reclaiming their time
- children laughing without fear
- adults dancing unapologetically
- entrepreneurs building from passion
- creators thriving in authenticity
- communities healing together

Joy is not trivial.
Joy is not superficial.
Joy is reconstruction.

Every time we choose joy, we rebuild our identity from the inside out.

Joy also plays a critical role in sustainability. Movements built solely on anger burn out. Identities built solely on resistance fracture. Joy provides fuel that can be renewed.

When joy becomes part of identity, people are more likely to protect their peace, maintain balance, and think long term. This matters for families, communities, and generational progress.

Joy is not the opposite of seriousness. It is the foundation of endurance.

REJECTING THE LIMITING NARRATIVES IMPOSED BY SOCIETY

We live in a time where media still tries to box us in — through stereotypes, headlines, and selective storytelling. But we are no longer swallowing those narratives whole. We are no longer accepting distorted images of ourselves. Black America has become more discerning, more conscious, more aware of the psychological games being played.

We are questioning how narratives are constructed.
We are interrogating who benefits from them.
We are creating our own media, our own platforms, our own stories.

This is how identity is reclaimed —
by refusing to let someone else hold the pen.

IDENTITY AS A GATEWAY TO FUTURE POSSIBILITY

Here's the deeper truth:
The future is created by those who have the courage to imagine themselves differently.

When a people rebuild their identity…

they rebuild their future.

Because identity determines:

- what we attempt
- what we expect
- what we believe
- what we tolerate
- what we pursue
- what we create

A possibility-based Black identity leads naturally to a possibility-based Black future.

This is why the rebuilding of Black identity is not just a cultural shift — it is a spiritual and psychological revolution that will define the next 100 years.

As identity reconstruction continues, it invites a deeper question, not just for individuals, but for the culture as a whole. Who do we become when we are no longer defined by what we survived?

That question is still unfolding.

But what is already clear is this: a people who redefine themselves from the inside out are no longer waiting for permission to live fully. They are moving with intention. They are building with clarity. They are shaping futures rather than reacting to histories.

CLOSING: A FUTURE AUTHORED BY US

For the first time in our history, Black identity is being rebuilt on our own terms. Not as a reaction to oppression, not as a response to stereotypes, not as a shield against trauma, but as an expression of who we *truly* are — brilliant, creative, resilient, spiritual, innovative, and free.

We are no longer inheriting an identity.
We are authoring one.
We are no longer accepting the narrative.
We are rewriting it.
We are no longer defined by the past.
We are stepping boldly into the future.

This rebuilding of identity is one of the greatest reasons the future belongs to us —
because the moment a people change the way they see themselves, the world is forced to follow.

And yet, as we step into this new identity, it is important to recognize that identity reconstruction is not simply an intellectual exercise. It is an energetic shift, a spiritual realignment, a reclamation of inner space that was once occupied by fear, doubt, and inherited limitation. Rebuilding identity means rewriting the internal scripts that have played in our minds for generations. It means choosing new beliefs to anchor ourselves to. It means giving ourselves permission to imagine beyond the boundaries of survival.

And that alone requires courage.

For so long, Black identity was shaped in environments where dreaming big could be dangerous. Where being too visible could be risky. Where ambition had to be measured, restrained, or hidden. Where opportunity had to be weighed against safety. These conditions shaped how our ancestors navigated the world — and those strategies were brilliant, necessary, and wise for the time in which they lived. But we are no longer living in their time. We are living in ours.

The challenge — and the gift — of rebuilding identity is understanding when to release the survival strategies of the past so they do not become the limitations of the future. Healing means acknowledging the brilliance of those who came before us while also embracing the freedom to author a new story.

This is why identity reconstruction is happening alongside emotional healing, spiritual awakening, and community empowerment. All of these movements are interconnected. You cannot step into a new identity if you are still holding onto a belief system built from trauma. You cannot expand your vision if fear remains quietly in the background, whispering that expansion is unsafe. You cannot embrace possibility while clinging to narratives designed to protect you from disappointment.

To rebuild identity is to trust yourself again.

It is to say:

"I am worthy of more than survival."
"I am capable of creating a life beyond what was modeled for me."
"I am allowed to want joy, peace, abundance, success, and ease."
"I am not defined by stereotypes, systems, or the wounds of history."
"I am more."
"I am whole."
"I am becoming."

This inner declaration is how identity shifts from trauma-based to possibility-based. And as more of us make that internal shift, we collectively create a new outer reality. Because identity and culture are mirrors — one shapes the other.

You can already feel this new identity emerging in the way Black people show up in the world. There is a softness where there was once armor. There is a confidence where there was once caution. There is a wholeness where there was once fragmentation. There is a spiritual depth where there was once emotional numbness. There is a joyful audacity — a willingness to pursue dreams that once felt out of reach, a refusal to dim our light for anyone's comfort, a boldness that says, "I am here, and I am enough."

This is the new Black identity: whole, expansive, intentional, conscious, and free.

The reconstruction of Black identity is not a trend — it is a transformation. And as it continues, it will reshape everything: our families, our communities, our institutions, and our future. Because once a people reclaim their identity, the world must adjust to the new truth they embody.

And that truth is simple:
We are no longer who they said we were.
We are who we choose to become.

"Without community, there is no liberation."

— **Audre Lorde**

CHAPTER 7

THE TRANSFORMATION OF THE BLACK FAMILY

Strength, Stability, Fatherhood, and New Foundations

One of the most powerful yet least discussed shifts happening in Black America today is the quiet transformation of the Black family. If you listen to mainstream media, outdated political talking points, or recycled stereotypes, you'd think the Black family is in crisis — fractured, unstable, dysfunctional, and on the decline. That's the story we've been fed for decades, repeated so often it has taken root in the national imagination.

But here's the truth the data reveals — and the truth many people don't want to acknowledge because it dismantles the narratives they are invested in maintaining:

The Black family is not collapsing.
The Black family is evolving.
The Black family is healing.
The Black family is transforming.

And much of that transformation is happening quietly, invisibly, outside the outdated storylines that America refuses to update.

This transformation is one of the strongest reasons the future belongs to us.

One of the reasons this transformation has gone largely unnoticed is that it does not conform to the spectacle-driven lens through which Black life is often viewed. Healthy families do not generate headlines.

Stability does not trend. Emotional growth rarely goes viral. But quiet transformation reshapes culture far more effectively than loud crisis ever could.

What is happening inside Black households today is not performative. It is intimate. It is happening in kitchens, living rooms, therapy sessions, and late-night conversations between partners who are choosing growth over avoidance. These shifts may not register on the evening news, but they are registering deeply in the lives of children who are growing up with more emotional literacy than previous generations ever had access to.

That is how real change takes root.

THE OLD NARRATIVE: A STORY THAT NEVER TOLD THE WHOLE STORY

The stereotype of the "broken Black family" has been one of the most powerful psychological weapons used against Black America. It has shaped policy, influenced public perception, undermined our self-esteem, and produced an internalized sense of inadequacy that many of us carry without even realizing it.

But that stereotype was always incomplete — and in many cases, intentionally distorted.

Because even in slavery, when families were torn apart on auction blocks, Black people recreated family wherever they stood. They built kinship networks through love rather than blood. They formed communities out of nothing. They raised each other's children. They healed one another through connection. They practiced a family structure rooted in resilience, not legality.

Black family has always been about heart over structure, connection over convention.

The narrative that the Black family is "broken" was never about the truth of who we are — it was about the assumptions of those who couldn't understand the depth and creativity of our bonds.

Today, the old narrative is collapsing because reality can no longer be ignored.

Another reason the old narrative persisted for so long is that it relied on narrow definitions of what family was supposed to look like. Those definitions were rooted in Eurocentric norms that never accounted for the adaptive brilliance Black communities developed under pressure.

When survival required flexibility, Black families adapted. When legal marriage was denied or disrupted, commitment still existed. When economic stability was intentionally undermined, mutual support filled the gap. When nuclear family structures were threatened, extended family systems expanded to absorb the impact.

What was labeled dysfunction was often innovation misunderstood.

By viewing Black family life through a rigid template, observers failed to recognize the strength embedded in adaptability. They mistook difference for deficiency. But difference is not absence of value. It is often evidence of creativity.

As that outdated template loses cultural authority, a more honest understanding of Black family life is emerging, one that honors function over form and love over legality.

THE NEW REALITY: BLACK FAMILY STRUCTURES ARE MORE DIVERSE, STABLE, AND INTENTIONAL

The modern Black family does not look like the 1950s American template — and thank God for that. Our families are more flexible, more adaptive, and more emotionally intelligent than ever before.

We see:

- Single mothers raising exceptional children
- Single fathers loving with tenderness and pride
- Married couples building wealth and stability
- Blended families thriving with intentional love
- Co-parenting models rooted in maturity
- Grandparents stepping in with wisdom and devotion
- Community families raising children collectively
- LGBTQ+ Black families nurturing safe spaces
- Young Black men becoming emotionally aware fathers
- Young Black women setting boundaries and standards
- Black couples prioritizing therapy, communication, and healing

This is not fragmentation.
This is evolution.

We are redefining family on our own terms — and we are doing it with love, creativity, and consciousness.

Intentionality is the key word here.

Modern Black families are not drifting into new structures out of confusion or collapse. They are choosing them consciously. They are asking better questions than previous generations were allowed to ask. Questions like: What does safety feel like? What does partnership require? What kind of environment allows children to thrive emotionally, not just survive materially?

This intentionality reflects a deeper level of self-awareness. It signals a shift from reactive decision-making to values-based living. When people choose family structures aligned with emotional health rather than social expectation, stability increases even if appearances change.

Stability is not sameness.
Stability is coherence.

And coherence is exactly what more Black families are cultivating now.

THE RISE OF THE PRESENT, ENGAGED BLACK FATHER

One of the most significant shifts — and one the media almost never highlights — is the rise of the engaged Black father.

Not the absent one.
Not the stereotype.
Not the lie.

The real Black father:

- the father at the playground
- the father at the recital
- the father at the parent-teacher meeting
- the father teaching emotional intelligence
- the father cooking breakfast
- the father praying with his children
- the father healing his childhood wounds so he doesn't pass them on
- the father who is present not just with money, but with heart

Black fatherhood is undergoing a renaissance.
It is tender.
It is grounded.
It is intentional.
It is beautiful.

And the data confirms it: **Black fathers are among the most engaged, hands-on fathers of any demographic in the country.** More diaper changing, more homework help, more physical affection, more day-to-day involvement.

This is not an accident.

This is consciousness evolving.

The rise of engaged Black fatherhood is also reshaping masculinity itself. Presence requires emotional availability. Nurturing requires vulnerability. Guidance requires patience. These qualities challenge outdated models of manhood that equated strength with distance and authority with silence.

As more Black men embrace fatherhood as a relational role rather than a performative one, they are rewriting what it means to lead within the family. Leadership is no longer defined by control, but by care. Authority is no longer expressed through fear, but through consistency and trust.

This evolution benefits everyone.

Children grow up with secure attachment. Partners experience shared responsibility. Men themselves experience deeper fulfillment because they are no longer suppressing parts of their humanity to fit inherited expectations.

Fatherhood, in this new context, becomes a site of healing rather than pressure.

HEALING THE WOUNDS THAT FRAGMENTED US

We cannot talk about the transformation of the Black family without acknowledging the trauma that shaped earlier generations. Slavery disrupted family structure by design. Jim Crow threatened the stability of every Black household. The economic manipulation of the 70s, the War on Drugs, and mass incarceration further destabilized family units in ways we are still healing from.

But we *are* healing.

There is a growing movement in Black America toward:

- therapy
- trauma awareness
- emotional intelligence
- conflict resolution
- co-parenting maturity
- generational healing
- conscious partnership
- spiritual grounding

Black people are learning:

"How do I avoid passing my pain to my children?"
"How do I teach love instead of fear?"
"How do I raise whole human beings in a world that once tried to break us?"
"How do I choose partners from a healed place, not a wounded one?"

This is transformation.
Not sudden.
Not perfect.
But undeniable.

One of the most profound shifts occurring alongside this healing movement is the willingness to talk openly about what was once unspeakable. Silence is no longer mistaken for strength. Avoidance is no longer framed as resilience.

Families are learning the language of emotional repair.

They are learning how to apologize without defensiveness. How to listen without preparing rebuttals. How to name harm without collapsing into blame. These skills are not innate. They are learned. And once learned, they transform family dynamics at a foundational level.

This emotional skill-building is quietly dismantling cycles that once felt inevitable. Patterns of abandonment, emotional withdrawal, and unresolved conflict are being interrupted not through force, but through awareness.

Awareness is the beginning of freedom.

BLACK LOVE IS EXPERIENCING A RENAISSANCE

Another beautiful shift is the rise of Black love — healthy, thriving, intentional Black love.

Not just romance.
But partnership.
Communication.
Healing.
Growth.
Accountability.
Emotional safety.
Shared purpose.
Shared vision.

You can feel it across social media.
You can see it in young couples redefining commitment.
You can hear it in the conversations happening in barbershops and beauty salons.
You can observe it in Black influencers, entrepreneurs, healers, and creators who are modeling a new way of loving.

We are unlearning the love scripts we inherited from trauma and writing new ones rooted in emotional truth.

Black love is not dying —
it is maturing.

This renaissance is also changing the timeline of relationships. More Black couples are choosing to move slowly, to prioritize emotional compatibility over urgency, and to build foundations before committing to lifelong partnerships. This patience reflects maturity, not fear.

It signals a collective understanding that longevity requires preparation.

By valuing emotional readiness as much as attraction, couples are reducing cycles of repetition and heartbreak. They are choosing to do the inner work before building shared lives, rather than expecting relationships to heal wounds they did not cause.

This shift is reshaping expectations around partnership. Love is no longer framed as rescue or completion. It is framed as collaboration. Two whole people choosing to grow together, not two wounded people hoping to be saved by connection.

As this mindset spreads, conflict is approached differently. Disagreement is no longer viewed as threat. It is viewed as information. Couples are learning that tension does not mean failure and that repair matters more than perfection. This emotional literacy creates stability that goes far beyond surface harmony.

Healthy Black love is also expanding beyond romantic partnership. It is visible in friendships, chosen families, mentorships, and community bonds that provide emotional nourishment and accountability. These relationships reinforce the understanding that love is not scarce and that connection does not have to be transactional to be sustaining.

This abundance mindset matters.

When people believe love is limited, they tolerate harm out of fear of loss. When they understand love as renewable and expansive, they set healthier boundaries. They choose alignment over attachment. They walk away from what diminishes them and invest in what allows them to flourish.

The renaissance of Black love is not about perfection or idealized images. It is about truth. Truth in communication. Truth in self-awareness. Truth in choosing partners and relationships that support growth rather than reinforce old wounds.

And as love matures within Black families and communities, it becomes a stabilizing force that extends outward. Children raised in environments where love is modeled as respectful, honest, and emotionally safe carry those lessons forward. They expect more. They demand more. And they create more sustainable relationships in every area of life.

This is how cultural change becomes generational.

Love learned in the home becomes leadership in the world.

And as Black love continues to evolve, it strengthens the foundation upon which the future is being built.

FAMILY AS AN ACT OF RESISTANCE AND AN ACT OF CREATION

For centuries, simply loving each other was an act of resistance. Raising children was an act of defiance. Protecting one another was an act of rebellion. Loving out loud was a challenge to a world that wanted us silent.

But today, the Black family is not only resisting —
it is creating.

Creating new models of partnership.
Creating new models of parenting.
Creating new ways of expressing affection.

Creating emotionally healthy environments.
Creating generational wealth.
Creating new legacies of strength and joy.

This creative energy is building a foundation for future generations that looks nothing like the instability of the past.

We are designing futures our ancestors would marvel at.

THE FUTURE IS BRIGHT BECAUSE WE ARE BECOMING WHOLE

The transformation of the Black family is one of the clearest signs that our future is bright. Because families — in whatever form they take — are the foundation of culture. When families heal, communities heal. When communities heal, identities heal. When identities heal, possibilities expand.

We are raising children with:

- higher emotional intelligence
- deeper cultural pride
- clearer self-awareness
- stronger boundaries
- more creative freedom
- more spiritual grounding
- more mental health literacy

These children will build the world we will one day inhabit.

And they will build it from a place of wholeness, not woundedness.

CLOSING: A FAMILY FOR THE FUTURE

The narrative of the "broken Black family" is outdated, inaccurate, and collapsing. What is emerging in its place is a dynamic, diverse, emotionally aware, spiritually grounded, and self-defined model of Black family life.

A family structure that is not fragile — but flexible.
Not broken — but reborn.
Not limited — but limitless.
Not constrained by the past — but creating the future.

The transformation of the Black family is one of the greatest reasons the future belongs to us.

Because the moment a people begin raising children from a place of healed identity and expansive possibility,
their cultural future becomes unstoppable.

And our future?
It is unfolding beautifully.

And yet, even as we celebrate this transformation, it's important to understand that the evolution of the Black family is not happening by accident. It is happening because we, as a people, are becoming more intentional than ever before. We are questioning the stories we inherited. We are challenging the patterns we absorbed. We are refusing to let the narratives of the past dictate the possibilities of our future. This is not a passive shift — it is an awakening.

The Black family is healing because Black individuals are healing. You can feel it in the conversations happening among men who once felt they had no permission to express vulnerability. You can feel it among women who are setting boundaries, reclaiming emotional space, and refusing to carry burdens alone. You can feel it in the way couples are approaching relationships with more honesty, transparency, and emotional accountability. You can feel it in the willingness of so many to break cycles that once felt inevitable.

There is a new softness in our community — a softness that does not signal weakness, but strength. A strength rooted in emotional safety, self-awareness, and love without conditions. The kind of strength our ancestors prayed for but rarely had the freedom to embody.

And this strength is reshaping the foundation of Black family life.

You see it when fathers hug their sons with tenderness because they want to give what they never received.
You see it when mothers apologize to their daughters because healing has replaced pride.
You see it when siblings talk about mental health openly, without shame.
You see it when men and women co-parent with maturity rather than resentment.
You see it when couples go to therapy *before* things fall apart instead of after.
You see it when families have conversations about generational trauma — not as blame, but as liberation.

This is the new Black family: honest, evolving, emotionally literate, spiritually grounded, and building futures from a place of intention rather than survival.

And this evolution is changing the cultural landscape in profound ways.

Because when children grow up in homes where emotional expression is allowed, where communication is modeled, where love is present, and where identity is affirmed… those children become adults who do not need to heal from their childhoods before they can step into their purpose. They become creators instead of survivors. They become leaders instead of reactors. They become visionaries instead of protectors of inherited wounds.

And that changes everything.

Every healed Black household is a revolution.
Every healthy Black partnership is a blueprint.
Every emotionally nurtured Black child is a prophecy.

The transformation of the Black family is not simply evidence of change — it is the engine of change. It ensures that the next generation begins their journey from a place further along the evolutionary path. They will not have to unlearn everything we had to unlearn. They will not have to fight the internal battles we had to fight. They will begin where we end — free, grounded, conscious, and whole.

And that is the true power of this moment.

The future looks bright not only because our families are healing, but because those families will raise children who already embody the consciousness we are still growing into. Children who will not inherit the same fears, wounds, limitations, or narratives we did. Children who will build from possibility rather than pain.

This is why the transformation of the Black family is one of the most profound reasons the future belongs to us.

Because the future is shaped in the home —
and Black homes are awakening.

"You can't use up creativity. The more you use,
the more you have."

— **Maya Angelou**

CHAPTER 8

THE RENAISSANCE OF BLACK CREATIVITY

Owning Our Stories, Shaping Culture, and Leading the Narrative

"Stop fighting for room at the table. Build your own table."
— *Tyler Perry*

There is a moment in every cultural revolution when the oppressed stop asking for permission and start creating their own platforms. When the ignored stop looking for validation and begin telling their own stories. When the unseen step into their own light, claim their own power, and build something the world can no longer deny.

Black America is living in that moment right now.

Tyler Perry's words are not just a quote — they are a declaration. A blueprint. A spiritual assignment. For centuries, Black creativity was filtered through the lens of gatekeepers who held the power to decide which of our stories mattered, which of our voices were "marketable," and which of our dreams were allowed to come to life. But today, the gatekeepers are irrelevant. We are not waiting for seats at their tables because we've learned to build our own — stronger, wider, more inclusive, more honest, more soulful, and infinitely more powerful.

This is the heart of the renaissance we are experiencing:
Black creativity is not just surviving — it is *sovereign.*

We are no longer fighting for space inside someone else's structure.
We are creating structures of our own.
We are no longer waiting for permission.

We are granting it to ourselves.
We are no longer trapped inside narratives that were never written for us.
We are writing our own with brilliance, courage, and audacity.

This renaissance is not accidental.
It is intentional.
It is the natural evolution of a people who have discovered that creativity is their birthright and ownership is their liberation.

What makes intention so powerful in this moment is that it represents a shift from reaction to authorship. For generations, Black creativity often emerged as response, response to exclusion, response to distortion, response to erasure. While that response produced extraordinary art, it also tethered creation to resistance.

What is happening now is different.

Black creators are no longer creating primarily to correct misconceptions or prove worth. They are creating because creation itself is an expression of alignment. The work is no longer anchored to what must be undone, but to what wants to be born.

This distinction matters.

When creativity is driven by alignment, it carries a different frequency. It feels grounded rather than urgent. Expansive rather than defensive. It invites participation instead of demanding recognition. And because of that, it travels further and lasts longer.

This is why so much Black creativity today feels effortless and magnetic. It is not chasing approval. It is radiating truth.

THE ERA OF GATEKEEPERS IS OVER

For generations, the creative industries were controlled by a handful of gatekeepers who decided:

- which Black stories "deserved" to be told

- which Black artists were "marketable"
- which Black voices were "acceptable"
- which expressions of identity were "safe enough"

But technology blew the gates off the hinges.

We now live in an era where a Black teenager with a phone can influence millions, where a Black creator with a laptop can launch a global brand, where a Black filmmaker can bypass Hollywood and still reach the world, where a Black musician can release an album without a label and top the charts.

Creativity is no longer filtered through permission.

We are our own greenlight.

And that is a dangerous thing for a society that once relied on controlling the narrative about us. When we control our stories, the stereotypes lose their power.

The collapse of gatekeeping has also shifted the psychology of the creator. When permission is no longer required, fear loses leverage. Fear thrives in systems where access is scarce and validation is external. But abundance dismantles fear at its root.

When creators know there are multiple paths forward, rejection loses its sting. When platforms are plentiful, experimentation becomes safe. When audiences can be reached directly, authenticity becomes an asset rather than a liability.

This psychological freedom is fueling risk taking across Black creative spaces. Artists are blending genres. Writers are defying categories. Entrepreneurs are building businesses that do not fit existing molds. The willingness to experiment signals confidence, and confidence accelerates innovation.

Innovation, in turn, reshapes culture.

THE RISE OF BLACK FILMMAKERS, AUTHORS, AND STORYTELLERS

Look around at the landscape of film, TV, and publishing. We are witnessing an explosion of Black stories across every medium:

- Love stories
- Sci-fi and futurism
- Spiritual narratives
- Historical epics
- Documentaries (like your *Shatter The Stereotypes*)
- Coming-of-age stories
- Business dramas
- Mental health journeys
- Joy-centered stories
- Black fatherhood stories
- Black womanhood stories

The spectrum of representation is expanding. We are no longer confined to trauma narratives. We are telling stories of joy, brilliance, complexity, and humanity.

And these stories matter because representation is not entertainment — it is identity formation.

A people who see themselves reflected accurately begin to think about themselves differently.

This is cultural healing.

Storytelling also shapes collective memory. The stories a society tells determine which lives are seen as meaningful, which experiences are normalized, and which futures feel imaginable. For too long, Black stories were framed through limitation. Even success stories were often framed as exceptions rather than expressions of capacity.

That framing is dissolving.

As Black storytellers gain control of narrative, they are expanding the emotional and intellectual range through which Black life is understood. Complexity is replacing caricature. Context is replacing assumption. Humanity is replacing abstraction.

This matters not only for Black audiences, but for the world. When a people are seen clearly, empathy deepens. And when empathy deepens, collaboration becomes possible.

Storytelling, then, is not peripheral to change. It is foundational.

MUSIC: THE GLOBAL LANGUAGE BORN FROM BLACK GENIUS

From jazz to blues, from hip-hop to R&B, from gospel to Afrobeats — Black people have created, shaped, or revolutionized virtually every major musical genre on Earth.

And now, Black musicians have something our ancestors never had: **ownership.**

We're seeing Black-owned:

- record labels
- distribution platforms
- festival brands
- streaming collectives
- publishing companies
- production studios
- independent performance networks

Artists aren't just performing the music — they're owning the rights, the masters, the infrastructure, the brand, and the legacy.

This is economic empowerment disguised as entertainment.

Music also carries memory in ways language cannot. Rhythm bypasses intellect and speaks directly to the nervous system. This is why Black music has always been a vehicle for emotion, spirituality, protest, and joy all at once.

What is changing now is agency.

Ownership allows artists to protect the integrity of their work across time. It ensures that cultural contributions are not extracted without compensation or context. It allows legacy to be passed forward rather than appropriated and diluted.

This shift from contribution to ownership represents a maturation of creative power. It transforms art from expression alone into infrastructure. Infrastructure sustains influence across generations.

FASHION: WHERE BLACK EXPRESSION BECOMES GLOBAL INFLUENCE

Black culture has shaped global fashion for decades — but today, Black designers, stylists, models, and creatives are finally being recognized as the innovators they've always been.

We see Black excellence in:

- high fashion houses
- luxury streetwear brands
- natural hair movements
- sustainable fashion
- accessories, jewelry, and design
- runway shows
- collaborations with global brands

This renaissance is not simply aesthetic. It is psychological.

Our style is an outward expression of inner liberation.

When we no longer shrink, we dress boldly.
When we no longer hide, we shine.
When we no longer fear judgment, we adorn ourselves with truth.

Fashion is also a form of language. It communicates identity before words are spoken. For Black people, fashion has long served as a site of resistance, pride, and self-definition. What is new is that fashion is now being paired with ownership, authorship, and intention.

Designers are no longer only shaping aesthetics. They are shaping narratives about beauty, professionalism, and value. They are challenging assumptions about who belongs in luxury spaces and what excellence looks like.

As these narratives shift, internalized limits dissolve. People begin to inhabit their bodies differently. They take up space. They express truth without apology.

This is embodiment as liberation.

DIGITAL PLATFORMS ARE AMPLIFYING BLACK BRILLIANCE

Perhaps the most powerful shift of all is the rise of digital entrepreneurship among Black creators. YouTube, TikTok, Instagram, podcasting, self-publishing, online courses, and global marketplaces have democratized creativity.

Black creators are using these platforms to:

- teach

- inspire

- entertain

- heal

- empower

- educate
- innovate
- build movements
- make money

We no longer need someone else's stage.
We build our own.
And our audience follows.

Digital platforms have revealed something truthfully profound:

When Black creativity is unleashed, people around the world respond with admiration, enthusiasm, and love.

The world *wants* what we create.

Digital platforms have also revealed something essential about audience behavior. When given the choice, people gravitate toward authenticity. They seek voices that feel real, stories that resonate emotionally, and creators who speak from lived experience.

This has dismantled the myth that Black stories are niche.

The global response to Black creativity shows that resonance is universal. Specificity does not limit reach. It expands it. When creators speak from truth, audiences recognize it instinctively.

This recognition builds trust. Trust builds loyalty. And loyalty creates sustainable ecosystems that do not depend on fleeting trends.

CULTURAL SOVEREIGNTY: WE ARE RECLAIMING OUR NARRATIVE POWER

For the first time, Black people are curating the narrative about Black people. We're not waiting for mainstream platforms to validate our stories. We're not begging for inclusion. We're not negotiating our worth.

We are leading the narrative.

And this matters because whoever controls the narrative controls:

- identity
- perception
- opportunity
- representation
- self-esteem
- cultural imagination

By reclaiming our narrative power, we are reclaiming the future.

Narrative power also shapes aspiration. When people see examples of success that feel attainable and aligned, they imagine themselves differently. They choose different paths. They take different risks.

This is how creativity becomes generational leverage.

Children raised in environments saturated with Black excellence internalize possibility as normal. They grow up expecting agency rather than accommodation. That expectation alone reshapes futures.

CREATIVITY IS OUR BIRTHRIGHT — AND OUR SUPERPOWER

The truth is, Black creativity did not survive slavery by accident. It survived because creativity is woven into the DNA of who we are. Our ancestors passed down rhythm, intuition, beauty, innovation, and spiritual expression as tools of survival, joy, and transcendence.

Today, that same energy is fueling a renaissance built on:

- ownership
- confidence
- visibility

- innovation
- authenticity
- self-expression

Creativity is not just what we do —
it is how we liberate ourselves.

Perhaps the most important implication of this renaissance is that it is self reinforcing. Each act of creation inspires another. Each success expands the horizon of what feels possible. Momentum builds quietly, then suddenly becomes undeniable.

This is not a peak. It is a trajectory.

Black creativity is not experiencing a moment. It is entering a sustained era of influence rooted in ownership, authenticity, and alignment. And because creativity is one of the primary engines of culture, this era will shape everything that follows.

CLOSING: A RENAISSANCE THAT RESHAPES THE WORLD

The renaissance of Black creativity is reshaping industries, transforming culture, and showing the world who we truly are — not through stereotypes, but through artistry, genius, and soul.

And this renaissance is only beginning.

The future belongs to us because the future will always belong to the creators.
To the innovators.
To those who imagine something new and dare to bring it into existence.

Black America is doing exactly that — boldly, brilliantly, and unapologetically.

This is our renaissance.
This is our time.
This is our moment.

And the world is watching —
not because they control our story,
but because they can no longer deny it.

And as extraordinary as this renaissance is, what makes it even more powerful is that it is happening organically. It is not being orchestrated by institutions or curated by mainstream gatekeepers. It is rising from the ground up — from living rooms, dorm rooms, garages, basements, community centers, bedrooms, and digital platforms across the world. It is fueled by authenticity, not approval. It is powered by freedom, not fear. It is spreading because brilliance cannot be contained, and truth cannot be silenced.

The renaissance we are experiencing is different from the Harlem Renaissance of the early 20th century — not because it is less profound, but because it is **more accessible**. It is not limited to writers, painters, or musicians. It is happening in science, in technology, in wellness, in spirituality, in social media, in entrepreneurship, and in fashion. The renaissance is not a moment; it is a movement. It is not confined to physical spaces; it is flowing across digital landscapes. It is not centered in one city; it is alive everywhere that Black people exist.

You can feel it in the way Black authors are writing books that transcend genre and expectation. You can feel it in the way Black inventors are creating technologies that solve global problems. You can feel it in the way Black entrepreneurs are launching companies rooted in purpose, community, and creativity rather than conformity. You can feel it in the way Black influencers are sharing wisdom, humor, beauty, and cultural pride with audiences in the millions. This is not a trend — it is a reclaiming of creative sovereignty.

What's even more profound is that this renaissance is happening in tandem with a shift in consciousness. Black creativity is no longer merely about producing art; it is about producing *alignment*. It is about creating from healed identities, from expanded awareness, from spiritual connection, and from an inner truth that says:

"I have something valuable to give to the world, and I no longer need permission to share it."

That is liberation.

Because when a people begin to create not from trauma but from truth, not from survival but from purpose, not from reaction but from intention — the world they build becomes radically different from the one they inherited.

And make no mistake: Black creativity today is not simply influencing culture; it is **reshaping the collective consciousness of humanity**. It is teaching the world how to be bold, how to be authentic, how to be soulful, how to be expressive, how to be expansive, and how to be unashamedly oneself. It is modeling resilience, joy, innovation, and spiritual depth in ways that transcend race.

This is why the renaissance of Black creativity is such an extraordinary reason to be optimistic about the future. Because creativity is not just art — it is identity. It is power. It is the ability to imagine something new and bring it into existence. It is the ability to redefine what is possible.

And a people who can imagine without limits are a people who will rise without limits.

The renaissance is here.
It is real.
It is unstoppable.

And it is reshaping the future in ways the world has not yet begun to understand.

"If you want a thing done right, do it yourself."

— **Madam C. J. Walker**

CHAPTER 9

THE SURGE IN BLACK WEALTH AND ENTREPRENEURSHIP

From Economic Survival to Economic Sovereignty

One of the most powerful and underreported transformations happening in Black America today is the surge in entrepreneurship, economic self-determination, and wealth-building. If you believed the mainstream narrative, you might assume that Black America is still at the margins of economic possibility — struggling, stagnating, or perpetually behind.

But that narrative is collapsing.

The truth is this:
Black entrepreneurship is not just rising — it is exploding.
Black-owned businesses are being created at some of the fastest rates in the country.
Black women are launching companies at a pace unmatched by any other demographic.
Black men and women alike are entering real estate, tech, consulting, e-commerce, creative industries, health, wellness, and finance in unprecedented numbers.

For the first time in generations, Black America is shifting from **economic survival** to **economic sovereignty** — and that shift is reshaping our future in profound ways.

WE ARE MOVING BEYOND THE OLD ECONOMIC SCRIPT

The "old script" for Black America — the one we were expected to follow — was rooted in limitation. Get a stable job, work hard, stay quiet, don't rock the boat, maybe retire with a little savings, and hope everything works out.

But younger generations are rejecting that script completely.

We are no longer interested in surviving the economy.
We are interested in *participating in it at the highest level.*
We are interested in ownership.
We are interested in equity.
We are interested in generational wealth.
We are interested in impact.

And we are realizing something revolutionary:

We have the power to build what we were once denied access to.

Black entrepreneurship is not simply a financial movement.
It is a psychological awakening.

At the heart of this awakening is a redefinition of self-perception. For generations, economic narratives positioned Black people as dependents within systems rather than architects of them. Even success was often framed as conditional or exceptional, rather than expected. That framing subtly shaped ambition.

What is changing now is expectation.

More Black people are entering economic spaces with the assumption that they belong there. They are no longer asking for permission to participate. They are arriving with vision, strategy, and confidence grounded in preparation. This shift in expectation alters behavior at every level, from negotiation to risk tolerance to long-term planning.

Expectation shapes outcomes long before results appear.

When people expect ownership, they seek assets rather than wages. When they expect growth, they invest in skills rather than settling for stability alone. When they expect longevity, they build systems rather than chasing short-term gains.

This psychological recalibration is foundational to the surge we are witnessing.

The rejection of the old script is not rooted in dissatisfaction alone. It is rooted in awareness. Awareness that economic systems were never neutral. Awareness that access was often deliberately restricted. Awareness that loyalty to a system that does not reciprocate is not virtue, it is habit.

Younger generations, in particular, are unwilling to confuse habit with wisdom.

They are asking sharper questions. Why should wealth only be accumulated through one narrow path? Why should creativity and intellect be separated from compensation? Why should economic security be delayed until late in life, if it arrives at all?

These questions are not radical. They are rational.

And rational questions demand new answers.

Those answers are increasingly found in entrepreneurship, ownership, and diversified income streams. Not because traditional employment has no value, but because dependence on a single source of income is no longer seen as safe or sufficient.

Economic intelligence has evolved.

THE RISE OF BLACK ENTREPRENEURS WITH VISION, PURPOSE, AND AGENCY

You can see this awakening everywhere you look:

- Tech founders creating apps, platforms, and software
- Consultants launching high-impact businesses
- Real estate investors building portfolios
- Financial coaches teaching wealth literacy

- Wellness practitioners monetizing healing work
- Creators turning influence into income
- Educators building online academies
- Podcasters scaling media brands
- Authors self-publishing bestsellers
- Black men and women entering new industries once closed to us

This is not isolated success.
This is a trend — a cultural wave of self-determination.

And behind that wave is a deeper truth:

The era of waiting for systems to include us is over.
We are building systems of our own.

What distinguishes this generation of entrepreneurs is not just innovation, but intention. Many are building businesses not simply to extract profit, but to solve problems they personally understand. This proximity to purpose creates resilience.

Purpose-driven businesses tend to endure.

When challenges arise, founders anchored in meaning adapt rather than retreat. They refine rather than abandon. They see obstacles as information rather than judgment. This mindset increases sustainability and long-term impact.

It also attracts aligned communities.

Customers are no longer just consumers. They are participants in shared values. They support businesses that reflect who they are and who they aspire to become. This alignment creates loyalty that advertising alone cannot manufacture.

The result is an ecosystem where economic success reinforces cultural affirmation.

BLACK WOMEN: THE NEW ECONOMIC POWERHOUSES

One of the most inspiring movements in this economic renaissance is the rise of Black women entrepreneurs.

Black women are:

- building companies with global reach
- breaking into industries once closed to them
- using creativity as capital
- turning passion into profit
- redefining leadership
- breaking generational cycles
- building communities through business
- running boardrooms and startups with equal mastery

Black women have always been innovators, organizers, nurturers, visionaries, and culture-shapers.
Now they are also becoming **wealth architects.**

This rise is not only shifting our economic landscape —
it is reshaping the cultural narrative of what power looks like.

The rise of Black women as economic leaders also reflects a convergence of skills that were historically undervalued. Emotional intelligence, adaptability, multitasking, and community building are now recognized as strategic assets rather than invisible labor.

These competencies translate powerfully into entrepreneurship.

Black women are building businesses that integrate profit with purpose, efficiency with empathy, and leadership with collaboration.

This integrated approach is proving especially effective in industries centered around wellness, education, media, and service.

As these businesses scale, they redefine leadership itself.

Leadership is no longer synonymous with domination or detachment. It is increasingly associated with clarity, care, and competence. This redefinition expands what power looks like and who it is allowed to include.

BLACK MEN ARE RECLAIMING ECONOMIC AGENCY

Black men, too, are experiencing a powerful shift. After generations of being boxed into narrow economic roles, we are redefining what it means to build, create, earn, and lead. We are launching companies in industries that once excluded us. We are investing, mentoring, partnering, and expanding economically in ways that previous generations could only dream of.

This is not about ego.
It is about agency.
It is about reclaiming the right to determine our destiny.

Economic empowerment is part of healing.
When Black men thrive economically, their families thrive.
When families thrive, communities transform.

Economic agency also alters masculine identity in profound ways. When Black men experience ownership and control over their economic destiny, it reduces the psychological toll of constant constraint. Stress shifts. Confidence stabilizes. Vision expands.

This has ripple effects beyond income.

Men who feel economically empowered are more likely to invest in family, mentorship, and community. They are more willing to think long term. They are more open to collaboration rather than competition rooted in scarcity.

Economic empowerment, then, becomes a stabilizing force that supports emotional health and relational integrity.

This is how wealth becomes holistic rather than extractive.

ACCESS TO KNOWLEDGE AND TOOLS IS DEMOCRATIZING WEALTH

One of the biggest reasons for the surge in Black wealth is simple: **the information gap is closing.**

Knowledge that was once hidden behind closed doors is now accessible online.

Black people are learning:

- how to invest
- how to build credit
- how to launch businesses
- how to acquire assets
- how to scale income streams
- how to use technology to create wealth
- how to leverage global markets
- how to negotiate and advocate for themselves

Financial literacy is no longer a luxury.
It is becoming part of our cultural language.

And with knowledge comes confidence.
With confidence comes action.
With action comes wealth.

The democratization of knowledge has also altered the pace of learning. What once took years of trial and error can now be learned in months. Mistakes are no longer hidden. Success strategies are openly shared.

This compression of learning time accelerates progress.

It also fosters accountability.

When information is accessible, excuses lose credibility. People are empowered to act, but they are also responsible for doing so. This balance between access and accountability strengthens agency rather than dependence.

Financial literacy is becoming cultural fluency.

And fluency changes behavior.

DIGITAL ENTREPRENEURSHIP IS THE GREAT EQUALIZER

In previous generations, starting a business required:

- capital
- physical space
- inventory
- credit
- gatekeeper approval

Today, all you need is:

- a phone
- an idea
- courage
- creativity
- consistency

The digital world has leveled the playing field in ways unimaginable even 20 years ago.

Black entrepreneurs are using:

- Shopify
- YouTube
- TikTok
- Instagram
- Online courses
- Self-publishing
- Print-on-demand
- AI tools
- Automation
- Subscription models

…to generate income streams that bypass systemic barriers entirely.

This is not a small shift.
This is economic liberation through innovation.

The democratization of knowledge has also altered the pace of learning. What once took years of trial and error can now be learned in months. Mistakes are no longer hidden. Success strategies are openly shared.

This compression of learning time accelerates progress.

It also fosters accountability.

When information is accessible, excuses lose credibility. People are empowered to act, but they are also responsible for doing so. This balance between access and accountability strengthens agency rather than dependence.

Financial literacy is becoming cultural fluency.

And fluency changes behavior.

WE ARE BUILDING WEALTH ON OUR OWN TERMS

Generational wealth is no longer a dream.
It is a plan.
It is a blueprint.
It is a strategy.
It is a movement.
It is the new normal.

Black families are:

- buying homes
- investing in real estate
- starting LLCs for their children
- building trust funds
- purchasing life insurance strategically
- investing in the stock market
- launching side hustles that become empires

We are no longer thinking only about survival.
We are thinking about legacy.

This is the energy of a people who have awakened to their power.

Building wealth on our own terms also means redefining success beyond accumulation. It means aligning money with meaning. It means using resources to expand freedom rather than replicate stress.

More Black families are having conversations about values alongside finances. They are asking how money can support health, education, mobility, and joy. They are designing lives rather than chasing symbols.

This alignment increases sustainability.

When wealth serves life rather than consumes it, it becomes a source of empowerment rather than anxiety.

Ultimately, the surge in Black wealth and entrepreneurship represents a convergence of awareness, access, and agency. Awareness of systemic limitation. Access to tools and knowledge. Agency to act without waiting for permission.

This convergence is rare in history.

When it occurs, it reshapes nations.

The economic awakening underway in Black America is not a momentary spike. It is a structural shift. One that will continue to compound across generations as knowledge, ownership, and confidence are passed forward.

CLOSING: ECONOMIC SOVEREIGNTY IS THE FOUNDATION OF A NEW FUTURE

The surge in Black entrepreneurship and wealth-building is not a trend — it is a transformation.

We are shifting from being consumers to creators, from employees to owners, from surviving within systems to building systems of our own.

Economic empowerment is not the only reason the future belongs to us — but it is one of the pillars that will sustain everything else.

Because when a people begin to control their economics…

they begin to control their destiny.

And Black America is stepping into that destiny with confidence, creativity, and unstoppable determination.

This surge is not just about money.
It is about freedom.

The freedom to imagine.
The freedom to build.
The freedom to choose.
The freedom to create a future that reflects who we truly are —
brilliant, innovative, resourceful, resilient, and unstoppable.

And yet, even with all of this extraordinary momentum, it's important to understand that the surge in Black entrepreneurship is not simply an economic movement — it is a **cultural awakening**. It represents a shift in identity, a shift in mentality, a shift in expectation. It reflects a generation of Black people who no longer wake up asking, "How do I survive today?" but instead ask, "What can I build today? What can I own today? What can I create today?" That shift alone is revolutionary.

We are witnessing a dramatic transformation in the psychology of Black America. The idea of wealth is no longer seen as something reserved for the privileged, the lucky, or the chosen few. Wealth — in all its forms — is becoming normalized in our collective consciousness. We are learning to speak the language of abundance rather than scarcity. We are learning to pursue opportunity rather than fear it. We are learning to see money not as a symbol of oppression, but as a tool for liberation, empowerment, and impact.

This shift in mindset is perhaps more important than the economic progress itself, because every financial transformation begins with a mental one. A person cannot build wealth if they subconsciously believe they are unworthy of it. A community cannot create prosperity if it still carries internalized narratives of limitation. What we are seeing today is a conscious rejection of those old narratives — and the birth of a new identity centered around possibility.

Part of this awakening is rooted in mentorship and representation. For the first time, millions of Black people can see — every single day — other Black men and women thriving as entrepreneurs, investors, CEOs, innovators, and wealth builders. Social media has made success visible. Podcasts have made information accessible. Books, online communities, masterminds, and virtual mentors have made guidance available. We are no longer isolated. We are connected — and connection accelerates growth.

There is also a spiritual component to this movement. Black entrepreneurs are not merely building businesses; they are building **purpose-driven platforms**. They are creating companies that uplift their communities, heal generational wounds, celebrate cultural identity, and provide services that were once unavailable to us. This is entrepreneurship as activism. Entrepreneurship as healing. Entrepreneurship as spiritual alignment. Entrepreneurship as destiny.

And as more of us step into that power, the ripple effects are enormous. When one Black business succeeds, it inspires others. When a Black entrepreneur hires employees, they create pathways for families. When a Black investor acquires property or assets, they shift the economic landscape of an entire neighborhood. When a Black creator monetizes their talent, they expand the definition of what's possible for the next generation.

This is how movements grow —
not from isolated victories,
but from shared belief.

And we are building a shared belief that **Black wealth is not the exception. Black wealth is the evolution.**
That is why this economic shift is unstoppable.
Because once a people taste agency, ownership, and the freedom to create their own future, they will never again accept the limitations of the past.

Black wealth is not a dream.
It is not a slogan.
It is not a fantasy.
It is the unfolding reality of a people finally stepping into their full power.

And that is one of the most compelling reasons the future belongs to us.

"Healing is not an overnight process.
It is a daily decision."

— **Iyanla Vanzant**

CHAPTER 10

THE MENTAL HEALTH REVOLUTION IN BLACK AMERICA

Healing the Wounds, Breaking the Silence, and Reclaiming Emotional Freedom

There is a quiet revolution happening in Black America — one that is not as loud as political activism, not as visible as entrepreneurship, not as celebrated as creative achievement. But it may be the most transformative revolution of them all.

Black America is healing.

For the first time in our history on this land, we are collectively doing the emotional, psychological, and spiritual work that our ancestors never had the freedom, safety, or resources to do. We are breaking generations of silence around trauma. We are dismantling the stigma around mental health. We are learning to name our wounds, understand our triggers, speak our truth, and seek support without shame.

This shift — this deep, internal evolution — is perhaps one of the strongest reasons why the future belongs to us.

Because when a people begin to heal from the inside out, their outer world cannot remain the same.

One of the most overlooked aspects of healing is that it fundamentally changes how power operates. Unhealed people are easier to manipulate because fear, shame, and unresolved pain cloud discernment. When emotional wounds remain unnamed, they become pressure points that can be exploited by systems, media, and narratives that thrive on division.

Healing removes those pressure points.

As Black people become more emotionally aware, they become harder to control through fear based messaging. They are less reactive. More discerning. More intentional about where they place their energy. This does not make them passive. It makes them precise.

Precision is power.

A community that understands its emotional patterns can interrupt them. It can pause before reacting. It can choose response over reflex. This is one of the quiet reasons this mental health revolution is so threatening to outdated systems. A healed people do not move predictably. They do not internalize imposed narratives. They think for themselves.

That kind of clarity cannot be legislated away.

WE ARE BREAKING THE GENERATIONAL PATTERN OF SILENCE

For decades, Black people were taught to "pray it away," "push through it," "be strong," or "keep it in the family." These coping strategies were born from necessity. When you live in a society that dehumanizes you, emotional suppression becomes a survival tactic.

But survival does not equal healing.

And now, for the first time, Black people are saying:

"I need help."
"I need to talk about this."
"I can't carry this alone anymore."
"My mental health matters."
"My emotions matter."
"I matter."

This is liberation.
Not political liberation.
Not economic liberation.
But **internal liberation** — the liberation of the psyche.

Silence was never neutral. It served a function. It protected people from further harm in environments where speaking carried risk. But silence also carried a cost. It isolated pain. It normalized suffering. It taught generations to endure without processing.

What we are witnessing now is the release of that cost.

When Black people speak openly about mental health, they are not rejecting strength. They are redefining it. Strength is no longer measured by how much pain one can carry alone. It is measured by the courage to seek support, to name truth, and to interrupt cycles that no longer serve growth.

This shift is especially significant because it changes what is modeled for future generations. Children who see adults talk openly about emotions learn that feeling is not failure. They learn that asking for help is not weakness. They learn that healing is part of living.

That lesson alone alters the future.

THERAPY IS BECOMING NORMALIZED — NOT TABOO

The fact that Black people are going to therapy in record numbers is groundbreaking. Not because therapy itself is revolutionary, but because **the willingness to be vulnerable is.**

Black men — who for generations were conditioned to see vulnerability as weakness — are now seeking therapy, joining men's groups, reading mental health books, practicing meditation, and learning emotional literacy.

Black women, traditionally expected to carry the emotional weight of families and communities, are finally receiving permission to place their healing at the forefront.

And young Black people are redefining emotional wellbeing not as an afterthought, but as an essential part of daily life.

We are finally giving ourselves what society never gave us — space to heal.

Normalization also reduces shame. Shame thrives in secrecy. It grows when people believe they are alone in their struggles. As conversations about mental health become more visible, shame loses its grip.

This visibility creates permission.

Permission to feel overwhelmed.
Permission to grieve.
Permission to rest.
Permission to set boundaries.

These permissions may seem simple, but they are revolutionary for a people historically denied rest, safety, and emotional autonomy.

The normalization of therapy also expands the definition of intelligence. Emotional intelligence is increasingly valued alongside academic and professional achievement. People are recognizing that self awareness, regulation, and empathy are not soft skills. They are life skills.

And life skills determine outcomes.

HEALING IS CHANGING HOW WE LOVE

When Black people heal emotionally, the entire ecosystem of our relationships shifts.

You see it in:

- marriages based on communication rather than obligation
- parents apologizing to children
- fathers expressing affection
- mothers releasing perfectionism
- couples practicing emotional attunement
- siblings breaking cycles of dysfunction
- families replacing shame with honesty

Love becomes deeper when fear is no longer shaping it.

Healing transforms our capacity to give and receive love.
It strengthens partnerships.
It expands empathy.
It makes room for softness, trust, and joy.

This internal shift becomes a cultural shift.

As emotional awareness grows, relationships become sites of growth rather than reenactment. Unhealed trauma often recreates itself in intimate spaces. Expectations go unspoken. Needs remain unmet. Conflict escalates because old wounds are triggered by present moments.

Healing interrupts this cycle.

People are learning to distinguish between past pain and present experience. They are learning to communicate needs without accusation and boundaries without withdrawal. They are learning that repair is more important than being right.

This shift changes family dynamics in profound ways.

Homes become places of safety rather than tension. Children grow up witnessing conflict resolution rather than conflict avoidance. Love becomes something that stabilizes rather than destabilizes.

That stability creates emotional capacity for creativity, leadership, and vision.

MENTAL HEALTH LITERACY IS BECOMING CULTURAL KNOWLEDGE

As a community, we are now familiar with terms like:

- trauma
- triggers
- boundaries
- self-care
- emotional regulation
- attachment styles
- generational wounds
- inner child work
- mindfulness
- anxiety
- depression
- healing journeys

These were not part of our vocabulary 20 years ago.

Today, they are part of our language — our conversations, our podcasts, our social feeds, our barbershops, our beauty salons, our church groups, our relationships.

This is what happens when a people evolve.

Cultural knowledge spreads differently than formal education. It moves through conversation, storytelling, music, humor, and shared experience. When mental health language enters cultural spaces, it becomes embodied rather than abstract.

This embodiment matters.

People begin to recognize their patterns in real time. They notice when boundaries are crossed. They name emotional responses as they arise. They become participants in their own healing rather than passive recipients of insight.

As this literacy deepens, it reduces internal conflict. People spend less energy fighting themselves and more energy creating aligned lives. This alignment increases efficiency, clarity, and resilience across every area of life.

Healing becomes practical.

SPIRITUAL AWAKENING AS A COMPONENT OF MENTAL HEALTH

Another remarkable shift is the integration of spirituality and emotional wellbeing. Many Black people are expanding beyond traditional religious frameworks into more holistic, universal, and personal expressions of spirituality.

This includes:

- meditation
- mindfulness
- breathwork
- energy healing
- journaling
- inner child practices
- affirmations
- somatic awareness
- yoga
- trauma-informed spiritual work

We are discovering that mental health and spiritual health are not separate.
They are intertwined.
They inform one another.
They support one another.

And as we heal spiritually, we heal psychologically.

This integration of spirituality and mental health represents a return rather than a departure. Long before modern psychology, Black communities understood the importance of mind body spirit connection. That wisdom was often dismissed or fragmented under colonized frameworks.

What we are seeing now is a reunification.

People are reclaiming practices that support nervous system regulation, self reflection, and embodied awareness. They are learning that healing does not only happen through analysis. It happens through presence. Through breath. Through stillness. Through reconnection with the body.

This holistic approach increases sustainability. Healing becomes something lived daily rather than something visited only in crisis.

HEALING IS EXPANDING OUR SENSE OF IDENTITY

A person who is healing begins to see themselves differently.
Not as a collection of wounds.
Not as a product of trauma.
Not as someone defined by pain.

Healing creates space for a new identity:

"I am worthy."
"I am whole."
"I am capable."

"I am lovable."
"I am enough."

This internal shift affects:

- our ambitions
- our relationships
- our boundaries
- our creativity
- our careers
- our ability to dream

A healed identity is an empowered identity.

Identity expansion also reduces internalized limitation. When people see themselves as whole rather than broken, they approach opportunity differently. They take risks with more confidence. They advocate for themselves more effectively. They tolerate less harm.

This does not make them rigid. It makes them clear.

Clarity is liberating.

It allows people to choose paths aligned with their values rather than defaulting to roles shaped by fear or expectation. It allows them to imagine futures not defined by reaction to past trauma.

This expanded identity fuels leadership.

CLOSING: HEALING IS THE FOUNDATION OF THE FUTURE

One of the most profound outcomes of this mental health revolution is that it is changing the emotional tone of Black life. There is more laughter that feels grounded rather than forced. More rest that feels earned rather than guilty. More conversations that feel honest rather than performative.

This tonal shift matters.

Tone shapes culture as much as policy. A culture that feels emotionally regulated can think long term. It can collaborate. It can innovate. It can plan.

Unregulated cultures remain stuck in crisis response.

Regulated cultures build futures.

When a people heal, they rise.
When they rise, they create.
When they create, they transform.
When they transform, they set a new path for future generations.

The mental health revolution in Black America is not just a trend — it is a rebirth.

We are honoring our pain without becoming it.
We are acknowledging our wounds without allowing them to define us.
We are releasing what no longer serves us and embracing a future rooted in emotional freedom and spiritual clarity.

This healing is the foundation upon which the future will be built — a future that belongs to us.

And even beyond all of this, perhaps the most powerful aspect of the mental health revolution in Black America is this simple truth: **we are finally giving ourselves permission to feel.** For centuries, feeling was a luxury we could not afford. When you live in constant danger, survival becomes the priority, not emotional introspection. When simply existing is an act of resistance, there is no space to process grief, fear, trauma, or exhaustion. But today, we are carving out that space — intentionally, courageously, unapologetically.

This permission to feel is not weakness.
It is evolution.

It is expansion.
It is evidence that we are no longer living in survival mode.

And with that shift, Black people are learning to ask deeper, more honest questions:

"How did my childhood shape me?"
"What patterns am I repeating without realizing it?"
"What generational wounds am I carrying?"
"What emotions have I suppressed?"
"What do I need in order to heal?"
"How do I want to show up in my relationships?"
"What kind of future do I want to create?"

These are the questions of a people who are awakening.
These are the questions of a people who are reclaiming their agency.
These are the questions of a people preparing to step into a higher version of themselves.

And as these questions are asked, something remarkable happens:
Our emotional bandwidth expands.

We begin to experience deeper joy because we are no longer numb.
We begin to experience peace because we are no longer carrying everything alone.
We begin to experience clarity because we are no longer clouded by unexamined pain.
We begin to experience love more fully because we have made space for it.

Healing is not simply the release of suffering —
it is the expansion of our capacity for life.

This internal opening has direct cultural implications.
A healed people raise healed children.
Healed children build healthier families.
Healthy families build stronger communities.

Strong communities shift the culture.
And once the culture shifts, the future shifts with it.

This is how healing works —
not in isolation,
but in ripples.

And Black America is rippling with healing energy right now.

You can feel it in the music.
You can hear it in the conversations.
You can see it in the art.
You can witness it in the therapy rooms, the church pews, the
meditation circles, the journals, the group chats, and the family
meetings.

We are not just surviving trauma —
we are metabolizing it.
Transforming it.
Turning it into wisdom, understanding, compassion, and power.

And this matters because a healed people cannot be manipulated by
fear.
They cannot be controlled by old narratives.
They cannot be diminished by stereotypes.
They cannot be boxed into someone else's limited imagination.

A healed people are dangerous —
not to society,
but to the systems that once relied on their woundedness.

A healed people reclaim their story.
A healed people reclaim their identity.
A healed people reclaim their possibilities.
A healed people reclaim their future.

And that is why this mental health revolution is one of the most
powerful reasons the future belongs to us —
because we are no longer carrying the past into the future.
We are entering the future from a place of emotional freedom,
spiritual clarity, and psychological strength.

And even beyond all of this, perhaps the most powerful aspect of the
mental health revolution in Black America is this simple truth: **we are
finally giving ourselves permission to feel.** For centuries, feeling
was a luxury we could not afford. When you live in constant danger,
survival becomes the priority, not emotional introspection. When
simply existing is an act of resistance, there is no space to process
grief, fear, trauma, or exhaustion. But today, we are carving out that
space — intentionally, courageously, unapologetically.

This permission to feel is not weakness.
It is evolution.
It is expansion.
It is evidence that we are no longer living in survival mode.

And with that shift, Black people are learning to ask deeper, more
honest questions:

"How did my childhood shape me?"
"What patterns am I repeating without realizing it?"
"What generational wounds am I carrying?"
"What emotions have I suppressed?"
"What do I need in order to heal?"
"How do I want to show up in my relationships?"
"What kind of future do I want to create?"

These are the questions of a people who are awakening.
These are the questions of a people who are reclaiming their agency.
These are the questions of a people preparing to step into a higher
version of themselves.

And as these questions are asked, something remarkable happens:
Our emotional bandwidth expands.

We begin to experience deeper joy because we are no longer numb.
We begin to experience peace because we are no longer carrying
everything alone.
We begin to experience clarity because we are no longer clouded by
unexamined pain.
We begin to experience love more fully because we have made
space for it.

Healing is not simply the release of suffering —
it is the expansion of our capacity for life.

This internal opening has direct cultural implications.
A healed people raise healed children.
Healed children build healthier families.
Healthy families build stronger communities.
Strong communities shift the culture.
And once the culture shifts, the future shifts with it.

This is how healing works —
not in isolation,
but in ripples.

And Black America is rippling with healing energy right now.

You can feel it in the music.
You can hear it in the conversations.
You can see it in the art.
You can witness it in the therapy rooms, the church pews, the
meditation circles, the journals, the group chats, and the family
meetings.

We are not just surviving trauma —
we are metabolizing it.

Transforming it.
Turning it into wisdom, understanding, compassion, and power.

And this matters because a healed people cannot be manipulated by fear.
They cannot be controlled by old narratives.
They cannot be diminished by stereotypes.
They cannot be boxed into someone else's limited imagination.

A healed people are dangerous —
not to society,
but to the systems that once relied on their woundedness.

A healed people reclaim their story.
A healed people reclaim their identity.
A healed people reclaim their possibilities.
A healed people reclaim their future.

And that is why this mental health revolution is one of the most powerful reasons the future belongs to us —
because we are no longer carrying the past into the future.
We are entering the future from a place of emotional freedom, spiritual clarity, and psychological strength.

"We are each other's harvest; we are each
other's business."

— **Gwendolyn Brooks**

CHAPTER 11

THE POWER OF BLACK COMMUNITY AND COLLECTIVE UPLIFT

Rebuilding What Was Broken, Strengthening What Remains, and Rising Together**

If you want proof that the future belongs to us, you don't have to look at statistics, economics, politics, or even social change. All you have to do is look at what is happening inside Black communities across the country. Something profound is unfolding — something that contradicts the narratives of fragmentation, division, and dysfunction that have been projected onto us for generations.

Black community is rising again.
Not in the same way it existed in the past.
Not constrained by the boundaries of neighborhoods or geography.
Not limited to blood ties or church memberships.

But rising through connection, through intention, through shared healing, through collective purpose, and through a renewed understanding that **we rise higher when we rise together.**

This resurgence of community is one of the most powerful reasons the future is bright — because the strength of a people has always been measured by the strength of its connections.

And Black America is reconnecting.

One of the reasons this reconnection feels so powerful is that it is not being driven by nostalgia. It is not an attempt to recreate a past that can never fully return. Instead, it is a reimagining of community suited for the world as it is now.

Modern Black community is adaptive.

It recognizes that people move, identities expand, and expressions of belonging evolve. Community is no longer defined solely by proximity, but by resonance. People are finding one another through shared values, shared healing goals, shared purpose, and shared vision.

This evolution matters because it allows community to remain alive rather than static. It allows connection to grow alongside consciousness. And it ensures that belonging does not require conformity, only authenticity.

COMMUNITY WAS ONCE ALL WE HAD — AND IT SAVED US

From the earliest days of our arrival in this country, community was our lifeline. It was our protection, our sanctuary, our source of identity, our emotional grounding, and our spiritual foundation. When everything else was stripped away — language, land, family, culture — we rebuilt the only thing we could rebuild: one another.

Black community has always been built on:

- shared struggle
- shared survival
- shared purpose
- shared hope

But it was also built on joy, on creativity, on humor, on innovation, and on a resilience so extraordinary that entire systems were created to suppress it.

And for generations, Black community endured — even under conditions where its very existence was a threat to the systems around it.

But today, something new is happening.

We are no longer building community just to survive.
We are building community to thrive.

Thriving requires a different infrastructure than survival. Survival focuses on endurance. Thriving focuses on sustainability. It asks different questions. Not just how do we make it through today, but how do we create conditions that allow future generations to flourish.

This shift is visible in the way Black communities are investing in long-term well-being. Mental health, financial literacy, wellness, education, and entrepreneurship are no longer treated as individual pursuits. They are increasingly approached as communal priorities. Knowledge is shared. Resources are pooled. Progress is measured collectively.

Thriving also requires trust.

Trust that cooperation produces greater returns than isolation. Trust that another person's success does not threaten your own. Trust that shared growth strengthens everyone involved. As trauma heals, trust expands. And as trust expands, community deepens.

This is how survival communities evolve into thriving ones.

THE FRAGMENTATION OF THE PAST IS HEALING

It's important to acknowledge that Black community has endured trauma. Redlining, mass incarceration, targeted disinvestment, gentrification, economic sabotage, and systemic disruption fractured neighborhoods, dismantled economic ecosystems, and separated families.

But healing has begun.

You can feel it in the way:

- Black professionals create peer networks
- Black parents form support groups
- Black entrepreneurs collaborate instead of compete
- Black men gather in healing circles
- Black women gather in empowerment spaces
- Black creatives share platforms and resources
- Black youth define community through identity, not geography

Something in our collective spirit is being restored.
We are remembering that **we were never meant to walk alone.**

THE RISE OF DIGITAL COMMUNITIES IS UNIFYING US GLOBALLY

Perhaps one of the most profound shifts in the last decade is the emergence of online Black communities — spaces where millions of Black people connect, heal, learn, and uplift one another without needing to be physically together.

We now have Black communities around:

- wellness
- entrepreneurship
- mental health
- spirituality
- parenting
- creativity
- relationships
- finance
- social justice

- technology
- personal growth

Digital communities have become the modern equivalent of the front porch, the barbershop, the beauty salon, the church foyer, the neighborhood block, and the family reunion.

They are places of belonging.
Places of affirmation.
Places of collective expansion.

And they are strengthening our cultural fabric in ways that previous generations could never have imagined.

What makes digital community so powerful is not the technology itself, but the intention behind its use. Technology becomes transformative when it is guided by purpose. In Black communities, digital spaces are increasingly being used to educate, affirm, organize, and mobilize rather than simply entertain.

These platforms are accelerating collective learning. Wisdom that once took decades to circulate is now shared in real time. Lessons learned in one city can immediately benefit people across the globe. This rapid exchange strengthens collective intelligence and shortens the distance between insight and action.

Digital connection also reduces isolation.

People who once believed their struggles were uniquely theirs now see reflections of themselves everywhere. They realize they are not alone in their questions, their healing journeys, or their aspirations. This recognition dissolves shame and replaces it with solidarity.

Solidarity creates momentum.

And momentum, when sustained, becomes movement.

COOPERATION IS REPLACING COMPETITION

A monumental shift is happening:
Black people are embracing collaboration as a form of empowerment.

We are learning that your success does not threaten mine.
Your achievement does not diminish mine.
Your elevation is not my loss — it is a win for all of us.

This shift is happening because trauma is healing.
Competition is a survival instinct rooted in scarcity.
Cooperation is a liberation instinct rooted in abundance.

And Black America is moving into abundance consciousness.

We see this in:

- partnerships between Black-owned businesses
- creators amplifying each other's platforms
- community-centered mentorship
- resource-sharing networks
- collective investment groups
- group-based real estate projects
- community healing movements

We are rediscovering our power as a collective.

Cooperation also changes how success is measured. Instead of focusing solely on individual advancement, success becomes relational. It is measured by how many people are lifted, how much knowledge is shared, and how much capacity is built within the community.

This reframing reduces burnout.

When people no longer feel they must carry everything alone, pressure decreases. Support systems distribute weight more evenly.

Collaboration allows individuals to contribute from their strengths rather than exhaust themselves compensating for weaknesses.

This is particularly important for long-term sustainability. Movements rooted in competition fracture over time. Movements rooted in cooperation adapt, regenerate, and endure.

What we are witnessing now is the early architecture of a more resilient Black ecosystem.

INTERGENERATIONAL CONNECTION IS STRENGTHENING

The gap between generations is closing. Younger Black adults are honoring the wisdom of elders, while elders are learning from the innovation and audacity of younger generations.

This exchange is sacred.

It means:

- culture is being passed on
- trauma is being healed
- traditions are being preserved
- new possibilities are being embraced
- wisdom is being applied to modern challenges

When generations talk to each other, learn from each other, and respect each other, the entire community becomes stronger.

Intergenerational connection does more than transfer wisdom. It restores continuity. When generations speak to one another, the community regains a sense of narrative coherence. Elders are no longer viewed only as reminders of struggle, and youth are no longer treated as problems to be managed. Each is recognized as essential to the present moment.

This recognition creates balance.

Elders offer perspective, patience, and historical grounding. They carry memory, not to anchor the community in pain, but to provide context for how far it has already traveled. They remind us that progress is possible because it has already occurred, often under far more difficult conditions.

Younger generations bring imagination, courage, and fluency in emerging tools. They are less attached to inherited limits and more willing to question assumptions that no longer fit the world as it is. Their willingness to imagine differently is not disrespect. It is evolution.

When these energies meet, growth accelerates.

Wisdom becomes relevant rather than static. Innovation becomes informed rather than reckless. The community moves forward without severing its roots. This exchange reduces generational resentment and replaces it with mutual respect.

And respect is the soil where collective strength grows.

THE RETURN OF MUTUAL AID, CARE, AND SUPPORT

Black mutual aid is not new; it is ancestral. But in recent years, it has resurfaced with renewed force.

We see it in:

- community-driven fundraisers
- grassroots support networks
- mental health support spaces
- food distribution efforts
- educational mentorship

- spiritual communities
- cooperative economics

This resurgence is proof that even as systems fail us, we refuse to fail each other.

Black community is not built on institutions.
It is built on intention.

One of the most powerful aspects of this resurgence of community is that it is reshaping how responsibility is understood. Responsibility is no longer framed as individual burden alone. It is shared. Distributed. Supported.

When communities function this way, people are less likely to fall through the cracks.

Someone notices when a neighbor is struggling. Someone reaches out when silence becomes concerning. Someone steps in when systems fail. This does not happen because people are forced to care. It happens because connection makes care natural.

This shared responsibility strengthens resilience.

It allows individuals to take risks because they know they are not alone. It allows healing to continue because support exists beyond crisis. It allows leadership to emerge organically because people are encouraged rather than isolated.

Most importantly, it changes what the next generation inherits.

They inherit a model of community that is alive, responsive, and rooted in love rather than fear. They inherit examples of cooperation rather than competition. They inherit proof that collective uplift is not an abstract idea, but a lived reality.

That inheritance matters.

Because futures are not built by individuals in isolation. They are built by communities that know how to support, challenge, and sustain one another over time.

CLOSING: A RISING COMMUNITY SHAPES A RISING FUTURE

Black community is becoming whole again — not in spite of our challenges, but because we have found new ways to connect, support, uplift, and empower one another. This collective healing is not just changing our experience in the present; it is reshaping the future.

A future where we celebrate each other.
A future where we invest in each other.
A future where we heal together.
A future where we grow together.
A future where we rise together.

The power of Black community is one of the greatest reasons the future belongs to us — because no people who stand in unity can ever be held down.

And Black America, after centuries of fragmentation, is standing together again.

And perhaps the most beautiful part of this resurgence is that it is not being orchestrated from the top down. It is not the result of government programs, institutional grants, or corporate initiatives — though those can help. The true renaissance of Black community is happening at the grassroots level, in the hearts, minds, and intentions of everyday people who are choosing connection over isolation.

It is happening in the brother who checks on his friend because he knows depression hides in silence.
It is happening in the sister who starts a healing circle because she knows women need space to breathe.
It is happening in the elder who mentors a young man heading down

a dangerous path.
It is happening in the entrepreneur who teaches financial literacy for free on weekends.
It is happening in the mother who refuses to let trauma define her parenting.
It is happening in the youth who creates a community garden to bring hope to their neighborhood.
It is happening in the spiritual communities embracing a broader vision of love, justice, and consciousness.

These small, intentional acts of connection are weaving a new cultural fabric — one made not of fear or fragmentation, but of belonging, healing, and love.

And here's the deeper truth: **Black community has always been strongest when built on love.**

Even in the harshest moments of our history, love was the glue that kept us together. Love was the strength behind our resilience. Love was the force that allowed us to endure the unbearable. Love was the compass that guided our survival. And today, as we heal from centuries of trauma, that same love is guiding our transformation.

This is why the resurgence of Black community is so powerful — because it represents a return to our true nature.
A return to connection.
A return to belonging.
A return to shared purpose.
A return to collective strength.

This new expression of community is also taking root in how we show up for one another's dreams. We are cheering each other's wins louder. We are buying Black, hiring Black, investing Black, promoting Black, supporting Black. We are embracing the principle that success multiplies when shared. We are redefining community not just as a social network, but as an economic and emotional ecosystem where everyone has a role, everyone has value, and everyone benefits from collective elevation.

And this shift has a ripple effect.
When Black communities become stronger, Black identities become stronger.
When identities become stronger, possibilities expand.
When possibilities expand, futures are rewritten.

This is why the evolution of Black community is not simply a cultural trend — it is a spiritual awakening.
It is a recognition that we are interconnected.
That our destinies are intertwined.
That no one rises alone.

It is the reclaiming of a truth that systems of oppression tried desperately to break:
We are powerful together.

And as we continue to build networks of support, knowledge, healing, and empowerment, we are creating a foundation that the next generation will stand on proudly. They will inherit a world where community is not something they must search for — it will be something they are born into.

This is why the future belongs to us.
Because a people united in purpose, grounded in healing, and connected through love cannot be stopped.

"I am because we are."

— **African Proverb (Ubuntu)**

CHAPTER 12

GLOBAL BLACK CONNECTIVITY

Why the Diaspora Is Becoming a Unified Force for the Future

For most of history, Black people across the world have shared a common origin but lived disconnected lives. Torn apart by slavery, colonialism, migration, borders, language, and imposed identities, we became a global people without a global conversation. Our stories were fragmented. Our struggles were localized. Our victories were often invisible to one another. And our power, though immense, remained largely untapped because it was divided.

That era is ending.

We are now living in the first moment in human history where Black people across the globe can see each other, speak to each other, learn from each other, collaborate with each other, and build with each other in real time. Geography is no longer a barrier. Distance is no longer a limitation. Borders no longer define belonging.

A global Black consciousness is emerging.

This connectivity is not accidental. It is the natural evolution of a people who were separated by force and are now reuniting by choice. And this reunion is one of the most powerful reasons the future belongs to us.

What makes this consciousness especially powerful is that it is forming organically rather than being imposed. There is no single institution directing it, no centralized authority controlling it, and no narrow ideology defining it. It is emerging from lived experience, shared curiosity, and a growing hunger for connection beyond inherited boundaries.

This organic quality gives the movement resilience.

When consciousness grows from the ground up, it adapts. It listens. It evolves. It reflects the complexity of the people it represents rather than forcing uniformity. This flexibility allows global Black connectivity to remain expansive rather than brittle.

It is not about agreement on everything.
It is about recognition.

Recognition of shared humanity.
Recognition of shared origin.
Recognition of shared destiny.

FROM SCATTERED TO SYNCHRONIZED

For generations, Black communities developed in isolation. African Americans fought for civil rights in the United States while Caribbean nations navigated post-colonial independence. African countries focused on nation-building while Black Europeans navigated identity in predominantly white societies. Afro-Latinos preserved culture while often remaining unseen.

Each group was strong. Each carried wisdom. But the lack of synchronization limited collective impact.

Today, that separation is dissolving.

A student in Atlanta can study African history taught by a scholar in Ghana. An entrepreneur in Lagos can collaborate with a technologist in Silicon Valley. A healer in Jamaica can guide a community in London. A filmmaker in South Africa can inspire an artist in Chicago. Ideas, culture, strategies, and solutions now move across the diaspora at the speed of light.

Across the diaspora, Black communities are exchanging knowledge on economic development, education reform, healing practices, cultural preservation, political organizing, technology, and entrepreneurship. Lessons learned in one part of the world are now informing solutions in another.

When African American communities discuss economic empowerment, they are learning from cooperative models in Africa and the Caribbean. When African nations consider cultural exports, they study how Black American music, fashion, and media influence global markets. When Black Europeans navigate identity, they draw strength from diaspora movements that affirm belonging beyond borders.

We are no longer reinventing the wheel in isolation.
We are building together.

Strategy requires perspective. It requires the ability to step back from immediate circumstances and see patterns across time and space. Global connectivity makes this possible.

By comparing experiences across the diaspora, Black communities are recognizing which challenges are local and which are systemic. This distinction matters because it informs response. Local challenges require tailored solutions. Systemic challenges require coordinated action.

This clarity prevents wasted energy.

Instead of reacting in isolation, communities can respond in alignment. They can apply pressure where it is most effective. They can support one another strategically rather than symbolically.

This is what transforms shared history from a source of pain into a source of power.

A NEW SENSE OF GLOBAL IDENTITY

This growing connectivity is doing more than sharing information. It is reshaping how Black people understand themselves.

Identity is expanding beyond nationality and into lineage. Beyond citizenship and into ancestry. Beyond skin color and into shared spirit.

Younger generations are especially fluent in this global identity. They listen to music from across the diaspora, follow creators from multiple continents, learn history that was never taught in school, and engage in conversations that were once impossible.

They are growing up knowing they belong to something vast.

That sense of belonging is not abstract. It is grounding. It creates confidence. It expands imagination. It allows young Black people to envision futures unconstrained by local limitations because they understand they are part of a global network of possibility.

A global identity does not dilute cultural specificity. It contextualizes it. It allows people to honor where they come from while understanding how they fit into a larger story.

This layered identity creates psychological strength.

People no longer feel forced to choose between local belonging and global awareness. They can hold both simultaneously. They can be rooted and expansive. Grounded and visionary.

This dual awareness reduces insecurity and comparison. It replaces competition with curiosity. Instead of asking whose experience matters more, people begin asking what can be learned from one another.

That shift alone deepens unity.

ECONOMIC AND CULTURAL POWER MULTIPLY WHEN UNIFIED

Global connectivity is also amplifying economic and cultural influence.

When Black creators, entrepreneurs, educators, and leaders collaborate across borders, scale becomes inevitable. Markets expand. Resources multiply. Cultural influence deepens. Innovation accelerates.

Diaspora collaboration allows Black-owned businesses to reach international audiences. It allows artists to draw inspiration from multiple traditions. It allows educators to share curriculum rooted in truth. It allows healers to blend ancestral wisdom with modern practice.

This is how global movements are built.
This is how generational wealth is sustained.
This is how culture becomes infrastructure.

Unified power also changes negotiating leverage. When Black creators and entrepreneurs operate collectively rather than in isolation, they gain influence. Markets respond differently to organized demand than to fragmented participation.

This is already visible.

Cross border collaborations are expanding audience reach. Joint ventures are increasing access to capital. Shared platforms are amplifying visibility. These collaborations are not merely symbolic. They are structural.

Structure sustains power.

As economic relationships strengthen across the diaspora, wealth circulation increases. Resources remain within communities longer. Knowledge is reinvested rather than extracted. This internal circulation builds resilience against external shocks.

HEALING ACROSS THE DIASPORA

Perhaps most importantly, global connectivity is enabling collective healing.

For the first time, Black people are having honest conversations across borders about trauma, resilience, spirituality, and identity. We are recognizing shared wounds without being defined by them. We are exchanging healing practices rooted in African spirituality, Caribbean wisdom, indigenous traditions, and modern psychology.

Healing is no longer isolated.
It is communal.

When one part of the diaspora heals, the vibration shifts everywhere. And as healing spreads, so does clarity, compassion, creativity, and confidence.

This healing is not about erasing the past.
It is about integrating it without carrying it as a burden.

Collective healing also deepens empathy across difference. When people recognize shared trauma without competing over pain, compassion becomes natural. This compassion reduces internal division and creates emotional safety.

Safety allows honesty.

Honesty allows growth.

As healing practices are shared across cultures, they evolve. They integrate ancient wisdom with modern understanding. They address the nervous system as well as the intellect. This holistic approach increases effectiveness and sustainability.

Healing becomes less about fixing what is broken and more about restoring what was always whole.

At its core, global Black connectivity represents a return to coherence. A remembering of self beyond fragmentation. A reclaiming of narrative authority that was once denied.

This coherence does not erase difference. It gives difference meaning within a larger whole.

And when coherence is restored, direction becomes clear.

A people who understand their interconnectedness move differently. They plan differently. They build differently. They recognize that the future is not something to wait for, but something to co create.

That understanding is now spreading.

THE FUTURE IS GLOBAL BY NATURE

The future does not belong to isolated nations or fragmented identities. It belongs to interconnected communities who understand their collective power.

Black people are uniquely positioned for this future because we have always been global. Our culture travels. Our influence spreads. Our creativity transcends borders. Our spirit refuses confinement.

Now, for the first time, our connectivity matches our reach.

Global Black connectivity is not a trend.
It is an awakening.

It is the reunion of a people who were separated by history and are now reuniting through consciousness. It is the realization that our strength has always been multiplied, not diminished, by our diversity.

And as we continue to connect, collaborate, heal, and build together, one truth becomes impossible to ignore:

The future does not belong to those who stand alone.
It belongs to those who stand connected.

And Black America, alongside the global Black diaspora, is stepping into that future together.

And there is something even deeper happening beneath the surface of this global reconnection.

What we are witnessing is not simply increased communication or collaboration. We are witnessing the **repair of a fractured memory**. For centuries, Black people were disconnected not only from each other, but from a coherent understanding of who we were before separation, before domination, before imposed narratives. Global connectivity is restoring continuity. It is allowing us to remember ourselves across time and space.

This remembrance matters because identity shapes destiny.

When a people see themselves as isolated, their imagination shrinks. When they see themselves as connected to something vast, ancient, and resilient, their sense of possibility expands. Global Black connectivity is restoring that expanded sense of self. It is reminding us that our story did not begin with oppression and does not end with limitation.

This reconnection is also dissolving false hierarchies within the diaspora. Old divisions — African versus African American, Caribbean versus continental, immigrant versus native-born — lose their power when people engage directly, human to human, story to story. Nuance replaces stereotype. Curiosity replaces assumption. Respect replaces competition.

What emerges is not sameness, but solidarity.

And solidarity does not require uniformity. It requires mutual recognition. It requires the understanding that different expressions of Blackness are not threats to unity, but expressions of it. Our diversity has always been one of our greatest strengths. Connectivity simply allows us to finally leverage it.

This matters profoundly for the generations coming next.

Children growing up today are inheriting a world where their reference points are no longer limited to their immediate environment. They can see excellence, leadership, innovation, and creativity reflected back to them from every corner of the globe. This exposure reshapes self-expectation. It normalizes greatness. It makes possibility familiar.

A young Black person who understands that they are part of a global network of thinkers, builders, healers, and creators moves through the world differently. They walk with a quieter confidence. They dream with fewer constraints. They carry less fear of invisibility because they know they are already seen.

In this way, global Black connectivity is not just changing how we relate to one another. It is changing how we relate to the future.

The future we are moving toward will be built by people who understand interdependence, who value collaboration over domination, and who recognize that progress is accelerated when knowledge, culture, and compassion flow freely. Black people, forged through centuries of adaptation and creativity under pressure, are uniquely prepared for this interconnected world.

We have always known how to survive together.
Now we are learning how to **thrive together**.

And as this global connection continues to deepen, it becomes increasingly clear that what once felt like fragmentation was only a pause. The reunion is underway. The circle is closing.

The diaspora is no longer scattered.
It is awakening.

And that awakening is one more reason, a powerful one, why the future belongs to us.

"The function of freedom is to free
someone else."

— **Toni Morrison**

CHAPTER 13

THE EXPANDING INFLUENCE OF BLACK LEADERSHIP

From Representation to Transformation, From Visibility to Vision

There is a new kind of Black leadership emerging in America — one that is not defined by titles, institutions, or traditional pathways, but by **consciousness, authenticity, and purpose**. This shift in leadership is one of the clearest indicators that the future belongs to us, because a people guided by elevated leadership cannot help but rise into their power.

For generations, Black leadership was shaped by necessity. We needed activists, organizers, defenders, protectors — individuals who fought against systems of injustice so that our most basic rights could be recognized. Their work was sacred, necessary, and life-saving.

But today, a different kind of leadership is emerging.
Not leadership rooted in resistance,
but leadership rooted in vision.
Not leadership shaped by trauma,
but leadership shaped by possibility.
Not leadership defined by fighting oppressive systems,
but leadership defined by building new ones.

This evolution in leadership is not just a shift in strategy — it is a shift in consciousness.

What makes this shift in consciousness so consequential is that leadership rooted in awareness produces outcomes that leadership rooted in urgency cannot. Urgent leadership reacts to problems as they arise. Conscious leadership anticipates problems before they harden into crises.

This anticipatory quality changes everything.

Leaders operating from awareness are less likely to replicate the very systems they seek to change. They are more attentive to unintended consequences. They listen more carefully. They move more slowly when needed, and more decisively when clarity arrives.

This type of leadership does not burn people out. It regulates them.

And regulated leadership creates environments where others can rise rather than collapse under pressure.

LEADERSHIP IS MOVING FROM THE FEW TO THE MANY

In the past, leadership often meant a single figure at the front of a movement. The face. The spokesperson. The one who bore the weight of a community's hopes and fears.

But modern Black leadership is decentralized. It lives in:

- teachers
- therapists
- entrepreneurs
- authors
- activists
- spiritual guides
- content creators
- thinkers
- community builders
- healers

- parents
- mentors

Leadership is no longer about personality — it's about purpose. And the more purpose-driven leaders we have, the stronger our future becomes.

We are entering an era where *every Black voice that speaks truth becomes a leader.*
Every Black person who heals becomes a leader.
Every Black person who breaks a generational pattern becomes a leader.
Every Black person who stands in authenticity becomes a leader.

Leadership is no longer limited to the stage.
It lives in the home, in the community, online, in classrooms, in boardrooms, and within every space where consciousness is rising.

Decentralized leadership also redistributes responsibility. When leadership is concentrated in a few visible figures, communities become dependent. When leadership is shared, communities become resilient.

Resilience emerges when people understand that their contribution matters.

This understanding increases participation. People stop waiting to be invited and start acting from internal permission. They recognize that leadership is not something bestowed. It is something expressed.

This shift is especially important for younger generations.

When leadership is modeled as accessible, young people are more likely to engage rather than withdraw. They experiment with responsibility earlier. They develop confidence through contribution rather than validation. And they learn that influence grows through service, not status.

This early engagement creates a pipeline of leaders who are emotionally prepared rather than prematurely elevated.

WE ARE MOVING BEYOND REPRESENTATION INTO INFLUENCE

Representation mattered — and still does.
Seeing Black faces in places where we were once excluded creates possibility in the minds of those who follow.

But representation is not enough.
Visibility does not equal transformation.

What we are witnessing today is leadership that not only fills the space,
but **reshapes the space.**

Black leaders are influencing:

- corporate culture
- mental health frameworks
- educational policy
- art and creative industries
- spiritual movements
- economic opportunity
- media narratives
- community structures
- public discourse
- technology and innovation

We are not simply being included.
We are redefining what leadership looks like.

Influence operates differently than representation. Representation changes perception. Influence changes behavior.

When Black leaders influence systems, they alter norms rather than merely occupy positions. They reshape policies, redefine success metrics, and shift the values that guide decision making. This level of impact is less visible, but far more durable.

Durability matters.

Temporary inclusion can be reversed. Structural influence compounds.

As Black leaders gain influence across sectors, they are embedding new assumptions into systems that will persist long after individual leaders move on. These assumptions include the importance of mental health, the value of community wellbeing, and the necessity of ethical leadership.

This is how cultural change becomes institutional change.

BLACK LEADERS ARE EMBRACING EMOTIONAL INTELLIGENCE AND CONSCIOUS LEADERSHIP

One of the most profound aspects of this new leadership is how emotionally intelligent it is. Today's Black leaders are:

- self-aware
- reflective
- heart-centered
- spiritually grounded
- trauma-informed
- inclusive
- visionary
- compassionate
- conscious of the collective impact of their choices

Gone are the days where leadership meant stoicism, suppression, or emotional isolation.
Today's leaders speak about healing, identity, purpose, community, and wellbeing.

Leadership has become more human — and therefore more powerful.

Emotional intelligence also protects leaders from becoming disconnected from the people they serve. Power has a way of insulating those who hold it. Emotional awareness counteracts that insulation.

Leaders who remain emotionally attuned are more likely to receive feedback without defensiveness. They are more willing to adjust course when harm is identified. They understand that leadership is not infallibility, but accountability.

This humility strengthens trust.

And trust is the currency of sustainable leadership.

When communities trust their leaders, they extend patience during uncertainty. They remain engaged during transition. They contribute ideas rather than withdrawing support. Trust transforms leadership from hierarchy into partnership.

OUR LEADERS ARE ROOTED IN AUTHENTICITY, NOT PERFORMANCE

This generation of Black leaders is not willing to code-switch their way into power.
They are not shrinking to be accepted.
They are not diluting their voice for approval.
They are not performing respectability for proximity to whiteness or institutional protection.

Instead, they are leading with:

- truth

- transparency

- cultural pride

- spiritual clarity

- grounded confidence

The unfiltered authenticity of today's Black leaders is dissolving the pressure to conform.
It is giving others permission to be themselves — fully and unapologetically.

A liberated leader liberates others.

Authenticity also reduces fragmentation within the self. Leaders who perform exhaust themselves. Leaders who lead from alignment conserve energy.

This conservation matters over time.

Burnout has ended many promising movements. Not because the cause lacked merit, but because the people carrying it were depleted. Authentic leadership reduces this risk by allowing leaders to show up fully rather than maintaining constant masks.

This openness invites collaboration.

When leaders are real, others feel safe bringing their full selves as well. This psychological safety increases creativity, honesty, and innovation within organizations and movements.

Authenticity, then, is not a personal preference. It is a strategic advantage.

WE ARE SEEING LEADERSHIP IN EVERY LIFE DOMAIN

One of the most inspiring shifts is that leadership is emerging in places we never saw it before.

We see Black leadership in:

- therapy rooms
- school districts
- HR departments
- wellness studios
- tech incubators
- nonprofit organizations
- spiritual centers
- community gardens
- motherhood and fatherhood
- social media platforms
- financial literacy movements

Leadership is no longer reserved for those in "positions of power." It is expressed through **impact**, not titles.

This democratization of leadership is expanding the influence of Black excellence across every dimension of life.

WE ARE PRODUCING LEADERS WHO BUILD — NOT JUST RESIST

Resistance will always be part of our story. But the leaders emerging today are builders.

They are:

- building institutions
- building communities
- building businesses
- building healing spaces
- building media platforms

- building creative ecosystems
- building wealth
- building families
- building consciousness

These leaders are not simply asking,
"What must we fight against?"
They are asking,
"What can we create?"
"What can we imagine?"
"What can we expand?"
"What can we build that will outlast us?"

This is legacy leadership.

Perhaps the most important implication of this expanding leadership is how it reshapes destiny. Leadership determines direction. Direction determines outcome.

A people led by fear will build defensive futures.
A people led by trauma will recreate struggle.
A people led by consciousness will build possibility.

The leadership emerging in Black America today is increasingly rooted in clarity rather than reaction. It is oriented toward creation rather than resistance. It is grounded in wholeness rather than survival.

This orientation will shape the next century.

It will influence how institutions are built, how conflicts are resolved, how children are raised, and how power is exercised. It will determine whether progress is extractive or regenerative, whether success is individual or collective.

And because leadership multiplies itself, this impact will extend far beyond the present moment.

CLOSING: THE FUTURE BELONGS TO THOSE WHO LEAD WITH CONSCIOUSNESS

The rise of this new leadership is not accidental.
It is a response to the needs of a changing world and a healing Black community.
It is a reflection of our evolution — spiritually, psychologically, socially, and culturally.

This leadership is powerful because:

- it heals
- it uplifts
- it unifies
- it empowers
- it expands
- it liberates
- it transforms

And as more Black leaders emerge — across industries, generations, and platforms — they will shape a future that is more just, more compassionate, more innovative, and more spiritually aligned than anything we have seen before.

The future belongs to us because **we are producing leaders who are prepared to guide it.**

Leaders with vision.
Leaders with integrity.
Leaders with emotional intelligence.
Leaders with spiritual grounding.
Leaders with purpose.
Leaders with heart.

Leaders who are not waiting for change —
but becoming the change.

And perhaps the most extraordinary aspect of this new wave of Black leadership is the fact that it is arising from a deep inner transformation rather than external pressure. These leaders are not motivated by ego, recognition, or validation; they are motivated by *alignment*. They are guided by an inner knowing that leadership is not a performance — it is a responsibility. It is not about being followed — it is about being of service. It is not about personal success — it is about collective elevation.

This shift from ego-driven leadership to purpose-driven leadership is one of the clearest signs that Black America is stepping into a new era. Because when leadership springs from consciousness rather than survival, its impact becomes exponential. A single leader rooted in presence, emotional intelligence, and spiritual clarity can influence thousands. They can shift culture not by force but by resonance. They can inspire change not through authority but through authenticity.

And this is exactly what we are seeing across Black communities worldwide.

You see it in the way Black men are stepping into leadership roles that embrace vulnerability rather than mask it. You see it in the way Black women are redefining leadership by integrating intuition, empathy, and creativity with intellectual rigor and entrepreneurial drive. You see it in the way young Black leaders are refusing to follow outdated models of power and instead creating entirely new frameworks based on collaboration, equity, mental health, and spiritual wellness.

In this new landscape, leadership is no longer limited to those with formal titles. A young Black woman speaking truth on TikTok is leading. A Black father breaking generational cycles is leading. A Black teacher showing up with compassion for their students is leading. A Black entrepreneur hiring within their community is leading. A Black healer creating spaces for emotional release is leading. A Black creator sharing wisdom is leading.

Leadership has become democratized — and in that democratization lies extraordinary power.

This accessibility of leadership also means that young Black children are growing up with a radically expanded concept of what a leader looks like. They are not confined to seeing leadership through the lens of politics, athletics, or entertainment. They see leaders who look like their mothers, their uncles, their neighbors, their teachers. They see leaders who look like themselves. This shift in representation reshapes internal narratives and expands horizons before limitations ever have a chance to take root.

And here is the deeper truth: **when a community produces leaders at every level, it becomes unshakable.**
It becomes resilient.
It becomes innovative.
It becomes future-oriented.
It becomes spiritually grounded.
It becomes socially powerful.

This is why the rise of Black leadership is such an essential reason the future belongs to us — because leadership is the steering wheel of a people's destiny. And for the first time in history, we are not only steering; we are designing the vehicle, building the road, and choosing the destination.

We are shaping the future rather than surviving it.
We are guiding the culture rather than reacting to it.
We are defining excellence rather than chasing it.

We are embodying the consciousness that will usher in the next era of Black evolution.

This is leadership not as performance —
but as spiritual purpose.

And with every new leader who emerges, the future grows brighter, stronger, and more aligned with the truth of who we are.

"Excellence is the best deterrent to racism or sexism."

— Oprah Winfrey

CHAPTER 14

THE INCREASING VISIBILITY OF BLACK EXCELLENCE

A New Narrative of Brilliance, Achievement, and Limitless Possibility

For centuries, Black excellence existed in the shadows — not because it was rare, but because it was *ignored*. The brilliance of Black minds, the creativity of Black artists, the resilience of Black families, the leadership of Black innovators, the genius of Black inventors, the courage of Black activists, and the sophistication of Black thinkers were often hidden behind the distortions of racism and the selective storytelling of a society that feared our power.

But today, the veil is lifting.

Black excellence is no longer hidden, minimized, or confined to footnotes.
It is visible.
It is undeniable.
It is global.
It is celebrated.
It is expanding across every domain of human achievement.

And this rising visibility is one of the strongest reasons the future belongs to us — because when a people begin to see themselves clearly, they begin to dream differently. And when a people dream differently, they create a future worthy of their brilliance.

VISIBILITY IS MORE THAN REPRESENTATION — IT IS VALIDATION OF IDENTITY

Representation matters, but what we are witnessing now goes far beyond simple inclusion. It is not just that Black people are showing up in places we were once excluded from — it is that we are showing up as ourselves.

We no longer have to contort, dilute, or shrink our brilliance to appease white comfort.
We no longer have to abandon our cultural authenticity to gain access.
We no longer have to hide our intelligence, creativity, or confidence to avoid stereotypes.

Black excellence today is:

- visible without apology
- powerful without permission
- expansive without limitation
- rooted in identity, not assimilation

This visibility is not just inspiring — it is paradigm-shifting.

BLACK EXCELLENCE IS THRIVING IN EVERY FIELD

Look around at any domain of human achievement, and you will find Black brilliance shining at levels unprecedented in American history.

We see Black excellence in:

- medicine
- engineering
- law

- astrophysics
- tech innovation
- entrepreneurship
- art and design
- film and media
- literature
- therapy and wellness
- education
- public policy
- corporate leadership
- spirituality

We are not confined to one lane.
We are not a monolith.
We are demonstrating excellence across the spectrum of human capability.

This diversification of achievement is critical because it expands what young people believe is possible for themselves.

BLACK EXCELLENCE HAS BECOME CULTURALLY INFLUENTIAL

For generations, Black culture has shaped America. But now, Black excellence is shaping global consciousness. The world watches us. Learns from us. Adapts to us. Celebrates us.

But Black excellence today is different from past eras — because it is rooted in ownership:

- Black directors directing Black stories
- Black authors writing global bestsellers
- Black CEOs leading Fortune 500 companies
- Black women commanding entire industries

- Black therapists transforming mental health
- Black creatives dominating digital platforms
- Black scholars elevating intellectual discourse
- Black entrepreneurs redefining business models

Excellence is no longer being extracted from us —
we are defining it, shaping it, and owning it.

VISIBILITY TRANSFORMS IDENTITY — INDIVIDUALLY AND COLLECTIVELY

There is a psychological revolution happening in Black minds across
the country.
When we see examples of greatness that reflect us, something
awakens.

A child who sees a Black astronaut begins to imagine outer space.
A teen who sees a Black therapist begins to imagine emotional
freedom.
A young woman who sees a Black entrepreneur begins to imagine
ownership.
A young man who sees a Black scholar begins to imagine
intellectual achievement.

Visibility expands imagination.
Imagination expands possibility.
Possibility expands destiny.

And Black destiny is expanding right now.

EXCELLENCE IS BECOMING NORMALIZED — NOT EXTRAORDINARY

Perhaps the most beautiful shift happening today is this:

Black excellence is no longer the exception.
It is becoming the expectation.

We are moving from:

- isolated accomplishments to generational momentum
- token breakthroughs to cultural transformation
- firsts to forevers

The narrative is no longer:

"Look at what this one Black person achieved."

Now it is:

"Of course Black people are achieving at this level."

This normalization changes everything.

OUR EXCELLENCE IS ROOTED IN AUTHENTICITY, NOT ASSIMILATION

The visibility of Black excellence today is not the visibility of the past.
It is not about fitting in.
It is not about being acceptable to the dominant culture.
It is not about conforming to someone else's standard.

It is excellence rooted in truth:

- wearing our natural hair
- speaking in our authentic voices
- honoring our cultural rhythms
- expressing our emotional intelligence
- embodying our creativity
- integrating our spirituality
- leading with our full humanity

Black excellence today is not polished for white approval —
it is grounded in Black identity.

That shift is seismic.

CLOSING: A VISIBLE PEOPLE BECOME AN UNSTOPPABLE PEOPLE

The increasing visibility of Black excellence is more than a social phenomenon — it is a spiritual affirmation. It is the universe reflecting back the truth of who we have always been: brilliant, capable, innovative, visionary, resilient, and limitless.

Our excellence was never missing.
It was only hidden.

Now it is rising.
And when a people begin to see their own brilliance reflected everywhere —
in media, in boardrooms, in classrooms, in leadership, in art, in science, in spirituality, in community —
their collective self-image expands.

And when identity expands, the future expands.

This visibility is not accidental.
It is intentional.
It is ancestral.
It is divinely orchestrated.
And it is one of the clearest signs that the future —
with all its possibility, potential, and promise —
belongs to us.

And yet even as Black excellence becomes increasingly visible, what's most powerful is the *foundation* from which it is emerging. This is not the kind of excellence that comes from striving to prove ourselves. This is not the excellence of exhaustion, perfectionism, or performance. This is not excellence rooted in a desperate attempt to counteract stereotypes or to make white society more comfortable with our existence.

The excellence rising today is **sovereign excellence** — the kind that comes from self-awareness, healing, and liberation. It is excellence expressed from within, not imposed from without. It is excellence grounded in authenticity rather than assimilation. And this distinction is what makes it so transformative.

Because for generations, Black people were told that excellence was the only way to justify our humanity. That we had to be twice as good just to be considered equal. That we had to earn the right to be respected. That we had to perform our value for an audience that was never willing to see us clearly.

But today, something deeper is happening.
Black excellence is emerging because Black people are finally recognizing our inherent brilliance, not because we need
 to prove it.

This shift in intention changes the emotional and spiritual vibration of our achievements.
It transforms excellence from a coping mechanism into a natural expression of our identity.

And this is why Black excellence today feels different — more expansive, more joyful, more aligned, more abundant, more communal. It is not being forced; it is being *revealed*.

You can feel this shift in the way Black people celebrate each other. There is a contagious joy in our collective pride. When a Black person wins, the entire culture celebrates. When a Black woman earns a doctorate, her sisters rejoice with her. When a Black man launches a successful business, his brothers uplift him. When a Black artist breaks barriers, entire communities feel seen. Our excellence no longer divides us — it unites us.

This unity is critical, because collective pride strengthens collective identity. And collective identity shapes collective destiny.

You can also see the expanding visibility of Black excellence in the subtle but powerful way that it affects our self-perception. When greatness becomes normal, self-limitation becomes harder to justify. When the bar is raised across a community, everyone is invited to rise with it. When children grow up surrounded by examples of brilliance, they internalize excellence as their default setting.

This is how cultures evolve — not from isolated accomplishments, but from shifts in collective consciousness.

And here's the deeper truth: **the visibility of Black excellence is not just a reflection of who we are — it is a prophecy of who we are becoming.** The more we see ourselves in positions of power, creativity, leadership, innovation, and influence, the more inevitable it becomes that future generations will surpass even our greatest achievements.

The world is witnessing Black excellence now because it has no choice. Our brilliance has expanded beyond the confines of invisibility. Our impact has grown too large, too constant, too powerful to ignore. And as this visibility increases, it creates an expanding cycle of inspiration, opportunity, empowerment, and transformation.

Black excellence is not a trend.
It is not a moment.
It is not a headline.
It is an unfolding revelation —
an unveiling of what has always been true.

And that revelation is one of the clearest signs that the future belongs to us.

What makes this era of visibility even more powerful is that Black excellence is no longer being framed as novelty. It is no longer treated as an anomaly that must be explained or justified. It is increasingly understood as a natural outcome of opportunity meeting preparation, creativity meeting access, and healing meeting self-belief.

This shift matters because novelty invites scrutiny, while normalcy invites sustainability. When excellence is framed as rare, it invites comparison and competition. When excellence is framed as expected, it invites participation. It signals to the collective that greatness is not reserved for a select few, but accessible to many.

And this reframing is quietly changing how Black people see themselves in everyday moments.

It changes how a student approaches a classroom, not as someone hoping to be noticed, but as someone who belongs. It changes how a professional enters a meeting, not with the weight of representation, but with the confidence of contribution. It changes how an artist creates, not with the fear of rejection, but with the freedom of expression.

These internal shifts compound over time.

The visibility of Black excellence is also disrupting one of the most damaging myths imposed upon us, the idea that success requires separation from community. For too long, achievement was framed as an individual escape rather than a collective ascent. The message was subtle but pervasive. To succeed, one must leave. To rise, one must distance oneself from those who are still struggling.

That narrative is dissolving.

What we are seeing now is excellence that reaches back. Excellence that builds platforms rather than ladders. Excellence that understands that true success expands capacity for others, not just status for oneself. Black excellence today is increasingly relational. It understands that the health of the individual is tied to the health of the community.

This is why so many successful Black leaders are investing in mentorship, education, mental health, and economic empowerment initiatives. They are not simply giving back out of obligation. They are acting from alignment. They recognize that their success is not separate from the collective story. It is an extension of it.

And this collective orientation strengthens the visibility of excellence even further.

When excellence circulates within a community, it multiplies. When knowledge is shared rather than hoarded, growth accelerates. When access is extended rather than restricted, innovation expands. This is how cultures build momentum that cannot be easily disrupted.

Another critical dimension of visibility is how it reshapes external perception without requiring internal compromise. In the past, visibility often came with conditions. Be visible, but not too loud. Be successful, but not threatening. Be exceptional, but not too authentic.

Those conditions are being rejected.

Black excellence today is visible on its own terms. It does not ask permission to exist. It does not negotiate its humanity. It does not soften its brilliance to be palatable. And because of that, it commands a different kind of respect.

Respect rooted in inevitability rather than approval.

This is especially evident in spaces where Black leadership was once rare or symbolic. In corporate environments, academic institutions, wellness spaces, and creative industries, Black excellence is no longer confined to diversity initiatives or isolated showcases. It is increasingly woven into the fabric of decision making, innovation, and thought leadership.

This integration matters.

When excellence is integrated rather than showcased, it shapes systems from within. It influences culture at the level of values rather than optics. And values determine outcomes long after attention fades.

The psychological impact of this shift cannot be overstated. Visibility does not simply inspire ambition. It stabilizes identity. It reduces the cognitive load of constantly navigating environments where one feels unseen or misunderstood. When people feel reflected, they expend less energy defending their existence and more energy expressing their potential.

This reclaimed energy is fueling creativity, leadership, and vision at unprecedented levels.

It is also changing how failure is interpreted. In environments where excellence is normalized, failure is no longer viewed as evidence of inadequacy. It is understood as part of growth. This reframing reduces fear and encourages experimentation. People take risks. They innovate. They stretch beyond familiar boundaries.

This willingness to risk is essential for future building.

Cultures that fear failure stagnate. Cultures that understand failure as feedback evolve.

The increasing visibility of Black excellence is cultivating a culture that understands evolution. One that is not frozen by past narratives or limited by inherited fears. One that recognizes that brilliance is not a finite resource, but a renewable one.

This is why excellence feels contagious right now.

It spreads through proximity. Through representation. Through conversation. Through celebration. When people see excellence embodied repeatedly, it becomes familiar. When it becomes familiar, it becomes believable. When it becomes believable, it becomes attainable.

And attainability changes behavior.

People pursue education differently. They invest in themselves differently. They set boundaries differently. They imagine futures that are broader, more complex, and more aligned with their inner truth.

The visibility of Black excellence is also correcting a long standing imbalance in how history is remembered and taught. For generations, Black contributions were framed primarily through struggle. Achievement was contextualized by oppression rather than brilliance. Innovation was overshadowed by adversity.

That framing is being corrected.

As excellence becomes visible across disciplines, history is being reread with clearer eyes. Contributions once minimized are being acknowledged. Narratives once distorted are being reclaimed. This correction does not erase struggle. It contextualizes it within a larger story of creativity, intelligence, and resilience.

This expanded historical lens strengthens cultural pride without requiring denial of pain. It allows for a more integrated identity. One that honors endurance while celebrating ingenuity. One that recognizes hardship without allowing it to define destiny.

And that integration is emotionally liberating.

When a people no longer have to choose between acknowledging pain and affirming greatness, they become whole. Wholeness creates stability. Stability creates vision. Vision creates futures.

This is why the increasing visibility of Black excellence is not simply a social milestone. It is a developmental one. It signals a culture moving from adolescence into maturity. From reaction into intention. From survival into sovereignty.

Sovereign excellence does not need constant validation. It does not posture. It does not perform. It simply expresses what is already true.

And what is becoming increasingly clear is that Black excellence has always been present. What is new is the collective willingness to see it, celebrate it, and build upon it without apology.

This willingness is reshaping not only individual lives, but the trajectory of the culture itself.

As visibility continues to expand, so will expectation. As expectation rises, so will participation. As participation increases, so will innovation. This cycle is already underway, and it is accelerating.

The future is being shaped not by isolated stars, but by constellations of brilliance. By networks of excellence. By communities that understand that visibility is not about being seen for its own sake, but about creating mirrors in which others can recognize themselves.

That recognition is powerful.

Because when people see themselves reflected in excellence, they do not ask whether they belong in the future. They begin asking how they will shape it.

And that question is the clearest indicator of all that the future, in every meaningful sense of the word, belongs to us.

"Our stories are our survival."

— **Bell hooks**

CHAPTER 15

THE GLOBAL RECOGNITION OF BLACK CULTURE AND INFLUENCE

From Margins to Mainstream, From Local Expression to Global Impact

There has never been a time in human history when Black culture has been more visible, more admired, more influential, or more globally impactful than it is today. What was once dismissed, ridiculed, appropriated, or ignored is now shaping the rhythm, style, language, technology, spirituality, art, creativity, economics, and imagination of the entire planet.

Black culture is no longer a subculture.
It is global culture.
It is a creative force that transcends borders, languages, and generations.

And this global recognition is one of the clearest signs that the future belongs to us — because culture is the soul of a people, and the world is now resonating with the soul of Black America.

What makes this moment so significant is that culture always precedes power. Before laws change, culture shifts. Before institutions evolve, imagination expands. Culture is the signal of what a society values, desires, and is becoming.

The fact that Black culture now resonates globally tells us something profound about the direction of human consciousness itself.

The world is not merely consuming Black culture because it is entertaining. It is resonating with it because it carries emotional truth.

It speaks to resilience in a time of uncertainty. It models joy in a world struggling with anxiety. It embodies creativity in an era hungry for originality. Black culture speaks to the human spirit in ways that transcend race, nationality, and language.

This resonance is not accidental. It reflects a deeper alignment between the wisdom forged through Black experience and the needs of a world seeking healing, meaning, and connection.

WE ARE NO LONGER BEING IMITATED WITHOUT BEING ACKNOWLEDGED

For decades, the world consumed Black creativity — our music, our fashion, our speech, our humor, our attitude, our aesthetic — without acknowledging the people who created it. Cultural appropriation was the norm, and global admiration rarely translated into respect.

But today, something has shifted.

The world is not just imitating Black culture;
the world is **crediting** Black culture.

From fashion houses to film studios, from international music charts to global beauty standards, from tech innovation to creative industries, the origin of our genius is finally being recognized.

We are not being copied;
we are being celebrated.
We are not being erased;
we are being centered.

This recognition changes everything.

Recognition changes power dynamics because it alters who gets to define value. For generations, Black culture was validated only after being filtered through non Black institutions. Success often required distance from origin, dilution of voice, or separation from community.

That era is ending.

Today, validation is increasingly coming directly from global audiences rather than centralized gatekeepers. People are choosing what resonates with them, and again and again they are choosing Black expression in its most authentic form. This shift returns narrative authority to the creators themselves.

When a people control their narrative, they control their future.

Narrative control influences opportunity, investment, collaboration, and legacy. It determines which stories are amplified, which voices are trusted, and which visions are funded. As Black creators retain authorship over their work, they are not only shaping culture, they are shaping the economic and psychological structures that surround it.

BLACK MUSIC IS THE SOUNDTRACK OF THE PLANET

Hip-hop is not just a genre — it is the most influential musical movement in the world.
Afrobeats is global.
R&B remains timeless.
Gospel continues to touch souls across continents.
Jazz remains foundational to modern music theory.

Black music is:

- studied

- analyzed

- sampled

- revered

- imitated

- globalized

And most importantly…
owned.

Black artists today are not just performers.
They are entrepreneurs, moguls, innovators, and cultural architects.

Music is just one example of where the world looks at us not with curiosity but with admiration — and often with awe.

BLACK STYLE IS SHAPING GLOBAL AESTHETICS

From streetwear to high fashion, from hair to beauty standards, from runways to social media, Black aesthetic influence is everywhere.

- Braids
- Locs
- Afros
- Melanin celebration
- Bold color palettes
- Streetwear couture
- Natural beauty movements
- Body positivity grounded in ancestral pride

Once stigmatized, our style is now revered.

The world doesn't just follow our fashion —
it follows our confidence.

BLACK CREATIVITY HAS BECOME A GLOBAL BENCHMARK

Whether it's digital innovation, storytelling, performance, comedy, filmmaking, dance, poetry, or content creation, Black creators have become global trendsetters.

Black culture sets:

- the tone
- the language

- the rhythm
- the energy
- the style
- the movement

Others follow and adapt.

This is cultural leadership.
This is influence born from authenticity, not assimilation.

Becoming a benchmark means others measure themselves against your standard. This is an extraordinary reversal of history. For centuries, Black creativity was judged against external norms that failed to recognize its brilliance. Now, Black expression is setting the norms others aspire to meet.

This shift has long term implications.

When Black creativity becomes the reference point, it influences how excellence is taught, evaluated, and rewarded. It reshapes education, media, and industry standards. It expands what is considered innovative, beautiful, intelligent, and valuable.

This influence is not limited to the arts. It extends into technology, leadership, communication, and problem solving. Black creativity carries an improvisational intelligence that thrives in complexity. In a rapidly changing world, that intelligence is not just admired, it is necessary.

BLACK SPIRITUALITY IS RESONATING ACROSS BORDERS

There is a global fascination with:

- African spiritual traditions
- Black meditation teachers
- Black mysticism

- ancestral wisdom

- Black approaches to healing

- soul-centered leadership

- embodiment practices

- emotional freedom grounded in spiritual awareness

The world is beginning to recognize that the soul-wisdom carried by Black people — particularly those descended from Africans — holds profound insights into healing, resilience, community, and human transformation.

Black spirituality is not being marginalized;
it is being honored.

SOCIAL MOVEMENTS LED BY BLACK AMERICA INFLUENCE THE WORLD

From civil rights to modern social justice movements, Black America's moral and spiritual leadership has inspired global movements for human rights, equality, peace, and liberation.

What begins in Black communities often becomes:

- global language

- global frameworks

- global consciousness

Black struggle has seeded global awakening.
Black resistance has inspired global courage.
Black resilience has modeled global transformation.

Now, the world not only watches us —
it listens to us.

Global influence also carries responsibility. When the world looks to Black America for moral clarity, it is because Black struggle has produced insight. Insight into injustice. Insight into resilience. Insight into the cost of dehumanization and the power of dignity.

This moral leadership does not come from perfection. It comes from lived experience.

Black communities understand what it means to demand humanity in systems designed to deny it. That understanding translates into movements that speak not only to Black lives, but to the universal longing for freedom, fairness, and belonging.

As these movements continue to shape global consciousness, they affirm a deeper truth. The lessons forged through Black experience are not marginal. They are central to humanity's evolution.

GLOBAL RECOGNITION EXPANDS GLOBAL OPPORTUNITY

As the world embraces Black culture, opportunities for Black creators, entrepreneurs, educators, and thinkers expand exponentially.

We now have:

- global markets
- global audiences
- global partnerships
- global platforms
- global distribution
- global influence

The world is not simply accepting us —
it is *seeking* us.

And when global demand meets Black creativity, brilliance, and leadership…
the future becomes limitless.

CLOSING: OUR INFLUENCE IS NOT AN ACCIDENT — IT IS DESTINY

The global recognition of Black culture is not a coincidence.
It is not a trend.
It is not a social experiment.

It is the natural unfolding of a truth that was always destined to rise:

Black culture is one of humanity's greatest gifts.

And now, the world finally knows it.

This global acknowledgment expands our power, our opportunity, our visibility, and our confidence. It opens doors that once felt impossible. It creates futures we were told not to imagine. It affirms what we have always known in our hearts:

We are brilliant.
We are influential.
We are creators.
We are architects of culture.
We are innovators of possibility.

And the world is now aligned with that truth.

This recognition is not the end of our story —
it is the beginning of a global evolution rooted in Black genius.

And that is yet another reason…
the future belongs to us.

Global recognition also invites a new internal posture. When excellence is reflected back consistently, it stabilizes self perception. It allows people to internalize belonging rather than constantly negotiate it.

This stabilization matters because confidence rooted in truth is different from confidence built on defiance. It is calm. It is grounded. It is expansive rather than reactive.

As Black people across the globe internalize this recognition, ambition becomes less defensive and more visionary. Dreams expand beyond survival and success into legacy, contribution, and creation. People begin asking not just how to succeed, but what kind of world they want to help build.

That question signals maturity.

And maturity is what turns influence into stewardship.

And yet, as extraordinary as this global recognition is, what makes it truly transformational is that it is grounded in **authentic Black expression** rather than manufactured personas. For the first time, the world is embracing us not when we mold ourselves into what *they* want us to be, but when we show up fully as who we *are*. That shift is monumental. It means that our brilliance, our creativity, our rhythm, our intellect, our spiritual depth, and our cultural genius are being valued on their own terms.

We are not being welcomed because we have learned to "fit in."
We are being welcomed because the world has learned to "tune in."

And as more of the world tunes into Black culture, something beautiful happens:
our global image transforms.

No longer are we seen solely through the lens of stereotypes or historical trauma.
No longer are our contributions dismissed or minimized.
No longer are we forced to justify our presence or explain our genius.

The world sees the truth — and the truth is luminous.

This global recognition also creates a profound psychological shift for Black people everywhere. When we witness our culture celebrated across continents, when we see our music filling stadiums, our dances inspiring millions, our style redefining aesthetics, our ideas shaping industries, and our leaders shifting global conversations, we internalize a powerful message:

"We belong anywhere on this planet."

This is not arrogance — it is liberation.

Because for generations, we were told explicitly and implicitly that we were limited to certain spaces, certain roles, certain narratives, certain expectations. But today, our global influence proves otherwise. There is no room we cannot enter. No field we cannot master. No vision we cannot manifest. No truth we cannot speak. No culture we cannot impact.

Our influence is not contained; it is expansive.
Not restricted; but accelerating.
Not localized; but planetary.

You can see this expansion in subtle yet powerful ways:

A young Black girl in London sees a Black American actress winning global awards and begins to rewrite the story she tells herself.
A Black boy in Ghana sees a Black entrepreneur from Houston building a global tech brand and begins to imagine his own possibilities.
A young woman in Brazil sees Black meditation teachers from the U.S. guiding global audiences and begins to explore her spirituality in a new way.
A teenager in Japan listens to Black American music and discovers a rhythm that resonates with her soul more deeply than anything else.
A boy in South Africa sees a Black NASA scientist interviewed by global media and begins to dream of exploring the stars.

These moments matter.
These moments multiply.
These moments create a global ecosystem of possibility.

And here is the truth the world is slowly waking up to:

You cannot contain a people whose culture has already circled the globe.
You cannot limit a people whose creativity shapes industries.
You cannot silence a people whose influence is global.
You cannot suppress a people whose identity is expanding.
You cannot deny a people whose brilliance is visible everywhere.

This global admiration is not simply praise — it is a mirror reflecting the truth of our power.

The world is evolving, and Black culture is a central force shaping that evolution.
The world is expanding, and Black creativity is guiding that expansion.
The world is awakening, and Black consciousness is helping open that awakening.

This is why the future belongs to us —
because the world has finally begun to align with our truth,
and the brilliance of Black culture is no longer ignorable, imitable, or containable.

It is universal.
It is unstoppable.
It is divine.

And it is rising.

"Freedom is never voluntarily given by the oppressor; it must be demanded."

— Dr. Martin Luther King Jr.

CHAPTER 16

THE NEW ERA OF BLACK POLITICAL POWER AND CIVIC ENGAGEMENT

From Exclusion to Influence, From Marginalization to Momentum

Black political power in America has undergone a transformation so profound that many people still don't fully grasp its implications. For generations, we were intentionally excluded from civic engagement — denied the vote, denied representation, denied voice, denied agency, and denied access to the systems that shaped the nation's future.

But the era of exclusion is ending.

A new era has begun — an era in which Black Americans are no longer fighting to be heard.
We are shaping the conversation.
We are influencing policy.
We are directing narratives.
We are mobilizing communities.
We are building coalitions.
We are shifting elections.
We are redefining leadership at every level of government.

This rise in political power is not superficial — it is systemic. It is cultural. It is generational. And it is one of the most powerful reasons the future belongs to us.

What makes this transformation especially significant is that it represents a shift from reactive participation to intentional engagement. For much of history, Black political involvement was driven by necessity, by the urgent need to resist harm or prevent further loss. While that resistance was essential, it often limited the scope of political imagination.

Today, that imagination has widened.

Black Americans are not only responding to injustice, they are proactively shaping policy agendas, long term strategies, and institutional priorities. This shift from reaction to design signals political maturity. It reflects a deeper understanding of how power operates and how it can be sustained over time.

Sustainable power is not built through urgency alone. It is built through vision, coordination, and patience. Those qualities are increasingly present across Black political spaces.

REPRESENTATION HAS EXPANDED BEYOND SYMBOLISM

There was a time when a single Black elected official was seen as a milestone. Today, representation is expanding so rapidly that it is becoming normalized rather than celebrated as an anomaly.

We see Black leadership in:

- Congress
- State legislatures
- City councils
- Mayoral seats
- District attorney offices
- Judicial appointments
- Educational boards
- Federal agencies
- Cabinet positions

But what's most transformative is that **these leaders are not tokens — they are change-makers.**

They are:

- writing legislation
- influencing national discourse
- reshaping criminal justice
- advocating for economic equity
- advancing education reform
- protecting voting rights
- elevating community voices
- leading with authenticity, not assimilation

Representation today is not symbolic.
It is functional.
It is strategic.
It is impactful.
It is powerful.

Functionality changes expectations.

When representation is symbolic, the burden is visibility. When representation is functional, the burden is effectiveness. Black leaders today are being evaluated not on whether they are present, but on what they produce. This shift raises standards and deepens accountability.

Accountability strengthens legitimacy.

As Black leadership becomes normalized, it also becomes diversified in skill and specialization. Leaders are emerging with expertise in law, economics, public health, education, environmental justice, technology, and urban planning. This breadth of competence allows Black political power to influence complex systems rather than remain confined to single issue advocacy.

Influence at this level reshapes outcomes.

It determines how resources are allocated, how priorities are set, and how communities experience governance in everyday life.

THE BLACK VOTE HAS BECOME A DECIDING FORCE

No political strategist in America can ignore the influence of the Black electorate.
We are not a footnote in political analysis —
we are the determining factor in countless elections.

Black voters are:

- informed

- organized

- mobilized

- strategic

- consistent

- influential

Elections at the local, state, and national level often hinge on Black turnout. And as civic engagement increases — particularly among young Black voters — this influence will only continue to expand.

Power is not simply given.
It is exercised.
And Black America is exercising it with sophistication and clarity.

Sophistication in political power also means discernment. It means knowing when to apply pressure and when to build alliances. It means understanding that progress often requires both principled resistance and strategic cooperation.

Black voters and organizers are demonstrating this discernment with increasing precision.

They are analyzing policy platforms. They are holding leaders accountable beyond election cycles. They are building coalitions that extend across race, class, and ideology without sacrificing core values. This strategic flexibility increases leverage.

Leverage matters.

Leverage allows communities to influence outcomes even when they are not numerically dominant. It transforms participation into impact. And it ensures that political engagement produces tangible results rather than symbolic victories.

BLACK POLITICAL LEADERSHIP IS BECOMING MORE DIVERSE AND MORE AUTHENTIC

We are no longer confined to a single type of political voice.
Black leaders today represent:

- progressives
- moderates
- conservatives
- independents
- activists
- intellectuals
- organizers
- coalition-builders
- entrepreneurs
- spiritual leaders

This diversity of thought strengthens us.
We are not a monolith — we are a mosaic.

And in that mosaic lies the power to shape the nation.

Authenticity is also becoming non-negotiable.
Black leaders today aren't performing assimilation.
They are leading from identity, integrity, and emotional intelligence.

That resonates.
That inspires.
That mobilizes.

Authenticity in leadership creates resonance. Voters respond not only to policy positions, but to coherence between values, words, and actions. When leaders speak from lived experience rather than scripted narratives, trust deepens.

Trust drives turnout.

Trust sustains movements.

As Black leaders lead from identity rather than assimilation, they model a form of power that does not require self erasure. This modeling has a ripple effect. It gives permission to others to bring their full humanity into civic spaces. It normalizes emotional intelligence, vulnerability, and moral clarity as leadership assets rather than liabilities.

This normalization is changing the emotional tone of politics itself.

GRASSROOTS MOVEMENTS ARE BECOMING POLITICAL POWERHOUSES

Some of the most influential political energy in Black America comes not from elected officials but from *us* — from the people, from the grassroots, from the community.

We see this in:

- voter registration drives

- organizing around mental health and trauma healing

- economic justice coalitions

- Black maternal health advocacy
- criminal justice reform movements
- HBCU activism
- youth-led civic initiatives
- spiritual and consciousness-based social change groups

These grassroots efforts have something institutions often lack:

- authenticity
- trust
- cultural connection
- moral authority
- emotional resonance

This is people-powered politics — and it is reshaping the landscape.

People-powered politics also expands political education. Grassroots movements are often the first places where individuals learn how systems work, how change happens, and how influence is built. These spaces cultivate leadership from the ground up.

Leadership development is no longer confined to elite institutions.

Community organizations are training voters, organizers, and candidates in real time. They are teaching strategy, communication, coalition building, and resilience. This distributed leadership model ensures continuity.

When leadership is cultivated broadly, movements do not collapse when individual leaders step away. Capacity remains. Knowledge stays rooted in the community.

That continuity is one of the strongest indicators of long term political power.

BLACK WOMEN ARE LEADING AMERICA INTO ITS FUTURE

There is no story of modern political power without acknowledging the brilliance, discipline, strategy, and resilience of Black women. They are the backbone of civic engagement, the architects of political turnout, the strategists behind electoral victories, and increasingly the leaders shaping policymaking itself.

Black women are:

- senators
- mayors
- governors
- judges
- movement leaders
- organizers
- policy experts

Their leadership is not emerging —
it is anchoring the political future of this country.

The anchoring role of Black women in political life also represents a shift in leadership style. It centers collaboration over domination, sustainability over spectacle, and long term impact over short term gain.

These approaches are particularly effective in times of complexity.

As social, economic, and environmental challenges intersect, leadership that integrates empathy with strategy becomes essential. Black women are modeling this integration at scale, demonstrating that strength and care are not opposites.

This leadership style is influencing how power is understood and exercised across the political spectrum.

YOUNG BLACK LEADERS ARE REDEFINING POLITICAL IMAGINATION

Perhaps the most exciting shift is happening among younger Black Americans who no longer see politics as an institution to fear or avoid — but as a platform for transformation.

Young Black leaders are:

- tech-savvy
- emotionally intelligent
- socially aware
- spiritually grounded
- collaborative
- future-focused

They are not asking, "How do we join the old system?"
They are asking, "How do we redesign it?"

This is visionary leadership.
And it is the future.

Visionary leadership requires imagination, and imagination thrives where fear has been addressed rather than suppressed. Younger Black leaders are entering political spaces with a different emotional relationship to power.

They are less burdened by internalized limitation and more comfortable questioning inherited assumptions. They see politics not as a rigid structure to navigate, but as a living system to evolve.

This orientation encourages experimentation.

It invites innovation in policy, communication, and engagement. It allows for solutions that address root causes rather than surface symptoms. And it expands what feels possible within the political arena.

CLOSING: OUR POLITICAL POWER IS EXPANDING BECAUSE OUR CONSCIOUSNESS IS EXPANDING

The rise in Black political power is not simply the result of demographic change.
It is the result of spiritual change.
Consciousness change.
Identity change.
Collective healing.

We are stepping into political influence with a clarity we've never had before:

- clarity about our worth

- clarity about our power

- clarity about our influence

- clarity about our purpose

- clarity about our future

A politically awakened people cannot be ignored.
A politically empowered people cannot be silenced.
A politically conscious people cannot be controlled.

And that is why this moment is not a peak —
it is a beginning.

We are not at the edge of our political influence.
We are at the foundation of it.

The future belongs to us —
because we are shaping it with intention, wisdom, power, and grace.

And yet the most powerful aspect of this new political era is not simply that Black people are entering positions of influence — it is the *way* we are entering them. We are stepping into political spaces not from a place of desperation or survival, but from a place of identity, purpose, and inner transformation. We are no longer trying to prove our humanity to a system that once denied it. We are walking into these spaces knowing exactly who we are, what we represent, and what our ancestors endured so that we could stand here.

This shift in consciousness changes everything.

A leader who knows their worth cannot be intimidated.
A community that knows its power cannot be marginalized.
A people who know their history cannot be misled.
And a generation that knows its purpose cannot be stopped.

Black political engagement today is different because it is rooted in self-trust.
We trust our voices.
We trust our values.
We trust our vision.
We trust our ability to shape the political landscape rather than simply endure it.

You can see this self-trust in the assertiveness of Black lawmakers who refuse to be silenced.
You can feel it in the strategic brilliance of Black organizers who mobilize voters with precision.
You can witness it in the courage of Black activists who speak truth to power without flinching.
You can hear it in the confidence of young Black leaders who are advocating for change that once seemed unimaginable.

And this evolution is speeding up, not slowing down.

As more Black people step into leadership roles, others begin to see themselves reflected in those positions. This creates a generational momentum — a psychological permission slip that says:

"If they can do it, I can do it too."

This matters deeply, because political power is not simply built through elections — it is built through belief.
Belief that your voice matters.
Belief that your vote matters.
Belief that your leadership matters.
Belief that your ideas matter.
Belief that your existence matters.

This belief is spreading through Black America like wildfire.

One of the most profound aspects of this moment is that political engagement is becoming integrated into everyday life. Civic responsibility is no longer limited to voting every few years. It is expressed through community involvement, mutual aid, public discourse, and cultural influence.

This integration strengthens democracy itself.

When people see governance as something they participate in rather than observe, accountability increases. Leaders are watched more closely. Policies are discussed more openly. Power becomes relational rather than distant.

This relational dynamic aligns with long standing Black traditions of collective responsibility and communal care. It brings political life closer to the values that sustained Black communities long before formal inclusion was possible.

But the rise in Black political power is not only about winning elections or securing positions. It is about transforming the *culture* of leadership itself. Black leaders are introducing emotional intelligence, spiritual depth, compassion-based governance, and trauma-informed policy-making. They are bringing their full humanity into political spaces that were once cold, detached, and mechanical.

This infusion of heart-centered leadership is critical — because the future will require leaders who can navigate complexity not just with strategy, but with wisdom. Leaders who understand the importance of healing as much as legislation. Leaders who recognize that policy must not only change systems, but must also uplift souls.

And Black leaders are uniquely equipped for this moment because our leadership is forged in empathy, resilience, creativity, and consciousness — qualities that the future of governance will desperately need.

This is why the new era of Black political power is such a powerful reason the future belongs to us. Because a people who have survived the harshest political exclusion are now shaping the nation with clarity, purpose, and strength. Because a community once denied a voice is now influencing the very fabric of democracy. Because a people once pushed to the margins are now holding the center with integrity, courage, and vision.

We are not simply participating in democracy.
We are redefining it.

And that evolution will echo for generations to come.

"The young people will determine whether or not we are going to survive."

— **Ella Baker**

CHAPTER 17

THE STRENGTH AND BRILLIANCE OF BLACK YOUTH

A Generation Unbound, Unafraid, and Unstoppable**

If you truly want to understand why the future belongs to us, look into the eyes of the young Black generation coming of age right now. They are not simply different from previous generations — they are operating on a new frequency entirely. They are bold in ways we weren't allowed to be. They are expressive in ways we were taught to suppress. They are conscious in ways many of us had to grow into. They are emotionally literate, spiritually curious, technologically brilliant, socially aware, and unwilling to inherit outdated narratives about their identity or their limitations.

Black youth are not the "leaders of tomorrow."
They are leaders **now** — reshaping culture, transforming industries, challenging systems, and redefining what it means to be young and Black in America.

And their strength, creativity, vision, and audacity are among the clearest signs that the future truly belongs to us.

What is especially important to understand about this generation is that their confidence is not performative. It is rooted. It comes from a deep internal alignment between who they are and what they believe is possible for them. This is a generation that has grown up with access to language, resources, and representation that allowed them to name their inner world earlier than any generation before them.

Naming creates power.

When young people can name their emotions, their boundaries, their values, and their aspirations, they are far less likely to be manipulated by fear or limited by inherited expectations. This self literacy gives Black youth an internal compass that guides them through uncertainty with clarity rather than confusion.

That clarity changes how they move through the world.

They do not ask for permission to exist fully. They expect it.

THEY ARE REJECTING LIMITING NARRATIVES BEFORE THEY TAKE ROOT

Unlike previous generations, who often internalized stories about inferiority, danger, or limitation, today's Black youth are rejecting those narratives entirely. They have grown up seeing:

- Black billionaires
- Black scientists
- Black therapists
- Black CEOs
- Black entrepreneurs
- Black artists dominating global charts
- Black athletes rewriting history
- Black activists shaping policy
- Black storytellers winning major awards
- Black creators influencing global culture

Visibility has changed identity.
Identity has changed expectation.
And expectation shapes destiny.

Where previous generations were taught to "keep your head down" or "work twice as hard to get half as far," this generation is saying something different:

"My brilliance is not negotiable."
"My identity is not a burden — it is a gift."
"My voice matters."
"My ideas matter."
"My creativity matters."

This is the mindset of possibility.

This early rejection of limiting narratives also means that shame has less opportunity to embed itself. Previous generations often carried silent burdens, internalizing messages about danger, deficiency, or disposability long before they had the tools to challenge them.

Today's Black youth are interrupting that process in real time.

They question narratives as they encounter them. They cross reference information. They seek community validation rather than institutional approval. And they are quick to discard ideas that do not align with their lived experience or inner truth.

This discernment is not arrogance. It is awareness.

Awareness protects identity. It allows young people to build self concept from affirmation rather than defense. And that foundation creates resilience that does not depend on external validation.

BLACK YOUTH ARE EMOTIONALLY AND SPIRITUALLY AWAKENING EARLY

One of the most remarkable aspects of this generation is their emotional and spiritual intelligence. They speak openly about:

- therapy
- trauma
- boundaries

- mental health
- burnout
- generational cycles
- spirituality
- purpose
- self-awareness

These were not conversations most Black adults were allowed to have growing up — let alone teenagers.

This early awakening means they are healing themselves before trauma calcifies.
They are breaking cycles at 16, 18, 22 that many of us didn't break until 30, 40, or 50.

That alone is revolutionary.

Early emotional and spiritual awakening also changes how young people relate to authority. They are less impressed by titles and more responsive to integrity. They are not easily persuaded by hierarchy alone. They look for alignment between values and behavior.

This has implications for education, leadership, and mentorship.

Adults who engage Black youth today must meet them with honesty rather than posture. They must be willing to listen as much as they teach. This mutual respect strengthens intergenerational relationships and allows wisdom to flow in both directions.

When youth feel seen rather than managed, they rise.

This dynamic creates environments where young people feel empowered to explore purpose rather than merely comply with expectation. Purpose driven youth become innovators rather than imitators.

THEY ARE TECHNOLOGICALLY FLUENT IN WAYS THAT REDEFINE POWER

Black youth understand technology not as a tool, but as a language — a native language. They are digital architects, creators, coders, influencers, designers, and innovators with unprecedented access to information, opportunity, and visibility.

They can:

- launch businesses from their phones
- build followings overnight
- produce studio-quality art in bedrooms
- shape public discourse with a single video
- build communities across the world
- access knowledge instantly

Technology has democratized creativity — and no one is leveraging that shift more powerfully than Black youth.

This gives them a kind of freedom no previous Black generation has ever experienced.

Technological fluency also means narrative fluency. Black youth understand that visibility is not accidental. It is constructed. They know how stories travel, how algorithms amplify voices, and how attention shapes influence.

This awareness allows them to use technology strategically rather than passively.

They curate identities with intention. They build platforms that reflect their values. They create content that educates, inspires, and mobilizes. This strategic use of visibility transforms technology into a tool of self definition rather than self comparison.

And because they understand reach, they understand responsibility.

Many young creators are deeply conscious of the impact their words and images have on others. This ethical awareness adds depth to their influence and signals a maturity often overlooked by critics who underestimate youth.

THEY CHALLENGE EVERYTHING — INCLUDING US

This generation does not accept "that's the way it's always been done."
And while that may frustrate older generations at times, it is one of the clearest signs of their brilliance.

They are questioning:

- gender norms
- beauty standards
- career expectations
- political assumptions
- religious structures
- educational systems
- workplace norms
- cultural belief systems
- mental health stigmas

This questioning is not rebellion — it is evolution.
It demonstrates a consciousness unwilling to live inside boxes built by someone else.

Black youth are not interested in fitting into outdated structures.
They are interested in transforming them — or building entirely new ones.

This challenge also extends inward. Black youth are willing to confront internalized beliefs within their own communities, even when doing so is uncomfortable. They question norms that normalize harm, silence vulnerability, or discourage emotional honesty.

This willingness to confront internal dynamics is essential for growth.

Evolution requires introspection. It requires the courage to examine not only external oppression, but internal patterns that limit expansion. Black youth are engaging in this work early, with clarity and compassion.

They are not rejecting elders. They are asking them to grow alongside them.

That invitation is an act of love.

THEY ARE EXPANDING WHAT BLACK IDENTITY CAN BE

One of the most profound shifts this generation brings is fluidity — not only in gender and sexuality, but in creativity, expression, spirituality, and ambition.

Black identity is expanding in directions that older generations were rarely allowed to explore.

Today's Black youth embody identities that are:

- multidimensional
- artistic
- spiritual
- entrepreneurial
- fluid
- community-focused
- globally connected

They are not asking for permission to exist in fullness — they are living it unapologetically.

Expansion of identity also reduces fragmentation. When people are allowed to exist in multiplicity, they no longer feel pressured to choose between parts of themselves. They can be intellectual and artistic. Spiritual and scientific. Soft and strong.

This integration creates psychological stability.

Stable identity supports healthy risk taking, creativity, and leadership. It allows young people to navigate complexity without losing coherence. In a world that is increasingly nonlinear, this capacity is invaluable.

Black youth are modeling what integrated identity looks like in real time.

THEY CARRY THE BRILLIANCE OF ANCESTORS WITH THE FREEDOM OF THE FUTURE

This generation is the bridge between what we survived and what we are becoming.
They carry ancestral brilliance in their blood.
They carry modern possibility in their minds.
They carry spiritual awakening in their hearts.
They carry boundless creativity in their hands.

They honor the past while refusing to be limited by it.
They see the present clearly while refusing to be defined by it.
They imagine the future boldly while actively **creating** it.

Black youth are not just inheriting the world — they are reshaping it.

This bridging role is sacred. Black youth are not rejecting history. They are translating it. They are taking ancestral wisdom and applying it to modern contexts with fresh eyes.

They understand that honoring the past does not require recreating its constraints.

By integrating ancestral resilience with modern tools and consciousness, they are creating pathways that did not previously exist. These pathways are not bound by fear. They are guided by possibility.

This synthesis is what allows progress to accelerate.

CLOSING: BLACK YOUTH ARE THE PROOF THAT THE FUTURE IS ALREADY HERE

The brilliance of Black youth is not potential energy — it is active energy.
It is happening now, every day, in every field, on every platform, in every community.

They are:

- leading movements
- building businesses
- expressing truth
- breaking cycles
- reshaping culture
- challenging the status quo
- stepping into consciousness early
- embodying authenticity fearlessly

They are not waiting for permission, validation, or approval.
They know who they are.
They know what they carry.
They know what they are capable of.

And they are showing us, with clarity and confidence, that the future belongs to us —
because they are already living it.

And what makes this generation even more extraordinary is their **fearlessness** — not the reckless kind, but the spiritually grounded kind. They move through the world with a deep internal knowing that their existence is purposeful, that their voices matter, and that their dreams are valid. They're not timid about their brilliance, nor are they apologetic about their ambition. They speak with a boldness many of us had to earn through decades of life experience and healing.

This is not accidental.
It is evolution.

These young people were born into a world where Black presidents, billionaires, moguls, scientists, filmmakers, and global superstars are visible and undeniable. They have grown up seeing Black excellence on the world stage, not as isolated anomalies, but as consistent realities. And when excellence becomes familiar, aspiration becomes natural.

This is why their dreams are bigger.
Their goals are bolder.
Their visions stretch beyond what previous generations even imagined.

They were raised on possibility.

And because they were raised on possibility, they move through the world expecting possibility — not as a miracle, but as a baseline.

You can see this confidence in the way Black youth express themselves creatively. They don't wait for gatekeepers to greenlight their ideas. They greenlight themselves. They don't wait to be chosen — they choose themselves. They don't wait for permission — they move forward with intention, clarity, and instinct.

This spirit of self-generated momentum is revolutionary.
It means that systems of oppression have less power to suppress them.
It means that limited narratives have less influence over their identity.
It means that they are building futures on their own terms.

Black youth also bring something else extraordinary to the table: **community consciousness.** They care deeply about justice, equity, mental health, spirituality, inclusion, identity, and the wellbeing of others. Their activism is not rooted in anger — it is rooted in empathy. Their calls for change emerge not from hatred of the past, but from love for the future.

This is a generation that wants to heal, not just protest.
To build, not just dismantle.
To create, not just critique.

They understand something profound:
that the world can only evolve when individuals evolve.

And they are evolving quickly.

They are also incredibly adaptive. Where older generations often struggled to keep pace with technological and cultural shifts, this generation embraces change intuitively. They think in networks. They innovate instinctively. They respond to disruption with creativity rather than fear. In a rapidly changing world, adaptability is one of the highest forms of intelligence — and Black youth have it in abundance.

But perhaps the most inspiring quality of this generation is their authenticity. They are not performing Blackness for anyone. They are not shrinking or contorting themselves to meet someone else's standards. They are not hiding their emotions, their spirituality, their identity, or their truth.

They are living in full color.

They are honoring the complexity of who they are.
They are embracing the freedom to explore.
They are refusing to inherit shame.
They are rejecting roles and expectations that no longer serve them.
They are defining themselves for themselves.

And because they are doing this at such a young age, they are setting the stage for a future where Black identity — in all its dimensions — is expansive, authentic, and empowered.

One of the clearest indicators of this generation's impact is how they are redefining success. Success is no longer measured solely by wealth or status. It is increasingly measured by alignment, impact, and wellbeing.

This redefinition is transformative.

When success includes mental health, purpose, and contribution, choices change. Careers are chosen with intention. Relationships are built with care. Boundaries are honored. Life becomes an expression rather than a performance.

This orientation will shape the future in profound ways.

Black youth are not the hope of tomorrow.
They are the evidence of today.
They are the living proof that the future is not just promising —
it is already unfolding.

The future being built by Black youth is not utopian. It is intentional. It acknowledges struggle without centering it. It honors history without being imprisoned by it. It embraces possibility without denying responsibility.

This balance is rare.

And it is precisely why this generation is so powerful.

They are not asking the world to save them.
They are showing the world how to evolve.

This is why the future belongs to us.
Because Black youth are not waiting for the world to change.
They are changing it.

"Education is the passport to the future."

— **Malcolm X**

CHAPTER 18

EDUCATION WITHOUT GATEKEEPERS

Knowledge, Technology, HBCUs, and the Democratization of Learning

There was a time when education for Black people was an act of rebellion.

A time when reading was illegal, curiosity was punished, and knowledge was withheld to maintain control. Even long after the chains of slavery were removed, access to quality education remained unequal, deliberately limited, and structurally sabotaged. For generations, our learning was mediated through institutions that often devalued our intellect and erased our contributions.

But today, something extraordinary is happening:

Knowledge has been liberated.

Education is no longer confined to classrooms, degrees, universities, or the approval of gatekeepers. Learning has become decentralized, democratized, and accessible in ways that previous generations could not have imagined. And this transformation is one of the most powerful reasons the future belongs to us — because knowledge is no longer locked behind walls we were never meant to enter.

We now live in a world where Black people can learn *anything*, from *anywhere*, at *any time*.

And that changes everything.

What makes this moment so historically significant is that education has always been one of the primary tools used to determine destiny. Whoever controlled knowledge controlled opportunity. Whoever restricted access controlled outcomes. For generations, Black people were forced to learn in environments that questioned our capacity, minimized our history, or attempted to shape our thinking rather than expand it.

The removal of gatekeepers dismantles that dynamic entirely.

When knowledge becomes freely accessible, learning is no longer dependent on permission. Curiosity becomes the only requirement. This shift is not simply technological. It is psychological. It restores agency to the learner and affirms that intelligence is not bestowed by institutions, but awakened through engagement.

This restoration of agency is one of the most profound shifts occurring in Black America today.

THE OLD MODEL OF EDUCATION IS CRUMBLING

The education system we inherited was built for a different era — an era of industrial labor, rigid hierarchy, and limited access. It rewarded memorization over creativity, obedience over curiosity, and standardization over critical thinking. It also reinforced racial inequities by underfunding Black schools, excluding Black scholars, and ignoring Black history.

But today's world doesn't reward conformity — it rewards innovation.
It rewards creativity.
It rewards problem-solving.
It rewards self-directed learning.

And Black learners are thriving in this new environment because they are naturally adaptive, intuitive, and self-motivated when barriers are removed.

The gatekeepers who once guarded knowledge no longer have the power they once wielded.

As the old model collapses, it reveals something important. The system did not fail Black learners because they lacked ability. It failed because it was designed to reward conformity rather than creativity and compliance rather than curiosity.

Black learners thrive when education becomes flexible.

When learning environments allow for exploration, experimentation, and self direction, Black brilliance surfaces naturally. This is because adaptability has always been a survival skill within Black communities. The same adaptive intelligence that sustained generations through constraint now fuels innovation when barriers are removed.

The crumbling of outdated educational structures is not a loss. It is an opening.

TECHNOLOGY HAS EQUALIZED ACCESS TO KNOWLEDGE

The smartphone — a device once dismissed as a toy — has become the most powerful educational tool ever created. Through it, Black people now have access to:

- world-class lectures
- online courses
- mentorship communities
- coding academies
- business education
- spiritual wisdom
- skill-based tutorials
- digital libraries
- global conversations
- creative learning experiences

Information that once required wealth or privilege is available to anyone with curiosity.

This democratization of knowledge is breaking generational cycles of limitation.
It allows us to bypass traditional barriers and learn at the speed of intention.

Technology has also changed the rhythm of learning. Education is no longer linear. It is iterative. People learn, apply, adjust, and refine in real time. This feedback loop accelerates mastery and reduces intimidation.

For Black learners, this matters deeply.

It allows learning to occur without the pressure of constant evaluation. Mistakes become part of the process rather than evidence of deficiency. Confidence grows through practice rather than approval. This environment nurtures resilience and curiosity rather than fear.

Learning becomes something people engage with willingly rather than endure.

HBCUS ARE EXPERIENCING A CULTURAL RENAISSANCE

Historically Black Colleges and Universities have always been sanctuaries of Black intelligence, culture, pride, and community. But today, HBCUs are experiencing a resurgence that is both cultural and spiritual.

More students are choosing HBCUs not because they lack options, but because they value:

- belonging
- mentorship
- cultural affirmation
- community
- legacy
- empowerment
- Black academic excellence

HBCUs are becoming innovation hubs in:

- STEM research
- business incubation
- social justice leadership
- digital technology
- mental health training
- cultural scholarship

They are not relics of the past —
they are engines for the future.

The resurgence of HBCUs also represents a reclaiming of intellectual lineage. These institutions were founded not simply to educate, but to affirm. They nurtured Black scholars when other institutions refused to do so. They preserved culture when erasure was policy.

Today, HBCUs are blending tradition with innovation.

They are honoring legacy while preparing students for a global, digital future. This balance provides students with both grounding and expansion. It allows them to develop competence without losing cultural coherence.

This model is increasingly recognized as a blueprint rather than an exception.

SELF-EDUCATION IS BECOMING THE NEW STANDARD

One of the most powerful shifts happening today is that Black learners are no longer waiting for institutions to tell them what to study or validate what they know. They are becoming:

- self-taught coders
- self-taught entrepreneurs
- self-taught healers

- self-taught creatives
- self-taught investors
- self-taught technologists
- self-taught content creators

This is not a rejection of formal education —
it is an expansion of it.

Self-education is empowerment.
It is agency.
It is liberation.

And it is becoming the new norm.

Self education also shifts responsibility inward. When learners choose their path, they become accountable for their growth. This accountability strengthens discipline and intention.

It also cultivates confidence.

People who teach themselves develop trust in their ability to learn anything. This trust transfers across domains. It fuels entrepreneurship, leadership, and creative risk taking. It replaces hesitation with initiative.

Self education is not solitary. It is self directed, but deeply connected to community.

KNOWLEDGE IS NOW A COLLECTIVE EXPERIENCE

Black learning today is not isolated.
It is communal.

We learn through:

- group chats
- digital communities
- mentorship networks

- online study groups
- podcasts
- social media
- webinars
- workshops
- spiritual collectives
- collaborative learning spaces

Black people are teaching each other in real time, sharing resources, exchanging insights, and democratizing knowledge with remarkable generosity.

This collective intelligence is accelerating our growth exponentially.

Collective learning also reinforces generosity as a cultural value. Knowledge is no longer hoarded as power. It is shared as empowerment. This generosity accelerates growth across the entire community.

When learning circulates, progress multiplies.

This shared intelligence reduces duplication of effort and shortens learning curves. It allows communities to move forward together rather than unevenly. This collective advancement strengthens resilience and cohesion.

Education becomes a shared victory rather than an individual achievement.

EDUCATION IS BECOMING ALIGNED WITH PURPOSE, NOT PRESSURE

Perhaps the most profound transformation is that Black people are no longer seeking education to simply "fit in," survive, or gain approval. We are seeking education that aligns with:

- our purpose
- our gifts

- our creativity
- our calling
- our spiritual path
- our entrepreneurial visions
- our leadership development

Learning is becoming personal, not performative.
Expansive, not limiting.
Liberating, not oppressive.

When education aligns with purpose, it becomes unstoppable.

Purpose aligned education also restores joy to learning. When people study what resonates with their gifts and calling, engagement deepens. Curiosity becomes intrinsic rather than forced.

This joy sustains effort.

People persist longer when learning feels meaningful. They integrate knowledge more fully. They apply it more creatively. Purpose driven education produces mastery that is both effective and fulfilling.

This alignment is redefining what success looks like.

CLOSING: EDUCATION WITHOUT GATEKEEPERS MEANS FUTURE WITHOUT LIMITS

The liberation of knowledge is one of the greatest revolutions of our time — and Black America stands to benefit immensely. We are no longer constrained by systems that once defined our intellectual worth. We are no longer dependent on institutions to shape our future. We are no longer waiting for validation from outdated structures.

We are educating ourselves.
We are educating each other.
We are educating the world.

And because of that, our future is wide open.

Education without gatekeepers means possibility without boundaries.
It means empowerment at scale.
It means creativity unleashed.
It means generation after generation rising higher.

This is why the future belongs to us —
because knowledge is finally free,
and so are we.

The internal shift taking place is perhaps the most revolutionary of all. When Black people see themselves as scholars by nature rather than exception, identity transforms. Learning becomes an expression of self rather than a response to judgment.

This identity shift dissolves inherited doubt.

It allows individuals to approach new fields with confidence rather than hesitation. It normalizes excellence. It reframes challenge as opportunity.

A people who trust their capacity to learn are no longer constrained by fear.

And yet, even with all the extraordinary transformations taking place in education, perhaps the most meaningful shift is the one happening internally. For the first time in our collective journey, Black people are beginning to see ourselves as the **primary architects of our own learning**. We are reclaiming the right to define what knowledge matters, how it should be taught, and who gets to be called a "scholar." This shift in identity is profound because education is not simply about acquiring information — it is about shaping consciousness.

When a people come to believe that they are capable of learning anything, mastering any skill, entering any field, or building any future, they become unstoppable. This internal shift dissolves the psychological residue of exclusion. It erases the illusion that educational excellence belongs to other groups. It reaffirms something our ancestors always knew but were prevented from expressing: **we are natural learners, innovators, thinkers, creators, and visionaries.**

You can see this awakening in the way Black individuals are rewriting their personal narratives. People who were once labeled "slow," "unmotivated," or "unfocused" in traditional schools are now thriving as entrepreneurs, designers, coders, healers, engineers, filmmakers, and change-makers. Not because they suddenly became smarter — but because they finally found learning environments aligned with who they are.

This is the gift of education without gatekeepers:
We no longer measure intelligence through systems never designed for our brilliance.
We no longer determine potential based on outdated academic hierarchies.
We no longer see ourselves through the distorted lens of standardized tests, biased teachers, or Eurocentric curricula.

We are learning in ways that honor:

- creativity
- intuition
- collaboration
- culture
- spirituality
- self-expression
- innovation

This kind of learning produces not just educated individuals, but **elevated individuals** — humans who are aligned with their purpose, connected to their community, and empowered to shape the world.

Another profound shift is the spiritual dimension of modern Black education. More and more, Black people are seeking knowledge that integrates intellect with intuition, fact with faith, information with inspiration. We are learning in ways that speak not only to the mind, but to the soul. This is why Black authors, spiritual teachers, consciousness leaders, wellness practitioners, and holistic educators are gaining unprecedented influence — because they offer wisdom that resonates with our humanity.

And as this spiritual and emotional literacy expands, Black learners are becoming more grounded, more self-assured, and more aligned. This alignment is what fuels long-term transformation. When learning flows from purpose rather than pressure, it becomes sustainable. When education uplifts rather than suppresses, it becomes liberating. When knowledge expands consciousness rather than reinforcing limitation, it becomes revolutionary.

And perhaps the most beautiful aspect of this new educational landscape is the sense of *collective uplift* it creates. Black people are not hoarding knowledge — we are sharing it. We are passing information across group chats, barbershops, beauty salons, social media, masterminds, workshops, churches, online communities, and family circles. This democratization of wisdom accelerates everyone. When one person learns, the entire community rises.

This is education as liberation.
This is knowledge as empowerment.
This is learning as destiny.

And it is one of the clearest signs that the future belongs to us — because a people who are free to learn are a people who are free to rise.

"You have to act as if it were possible to radically transform the world."

— **Angela Davis**

CHAPTER 19

THE MENTAL, EMOTIONAL, AND SPIRITUAL TRANSFORMATION MOVEMENT

Healing the Past, Elevating the Present, and Awakening the Future Self

There is a revolution taking place within Black America, one that is quieter than protests, deeper than politics, and more powerful than legislation. It is happening in living rooms and meditation circles, therapy sessions and barbershops, church altars and journaling spaces, online communities and sacred conversations. It is an inner revolution, a transformation of mind, emotion, and spirit that is reshaping what it means to be Black in the 21st century.

This movement is not about survival, it is about evolution.
It is not about coping, it is about awakening.
It is not about enduring, it is about transcending.

For the first time in our collective journey, Black people are healing at scale.
Healing from generational trauma.
Healing from societal conditioning.
Healing from internalized narratives.
Healing from inherited wounds.
Healing from systems that worked against our brilliance.

This movement is fundamentally shifting our collective identity, and it is one of the most powerful reasons the future belongs to us.

What makes this shift so unprecedented is that it is not being driven by crisis alone. Historically, transformation within Black America has

269

often been catalyzed by external pressure, violence, or urgent threat. While those moments produced courage and resilience, they rarely allowed for sustained inner work.

This moment is different.

The transformation underway is being driven by choice rather than coercion. Black people are choosing to heal even when survival no longer demands constant vigilance. This choice signals an evolutionary step in consciousness. It reflects a community that is no longer defined solely by reaction, but by intention.

Intention changes trajectory.

When healing is chosen rather than forced, it integrates more deeply. It becomes identity rather than intervention. It reshapes how people see themselves not as damaged or broken, but as whole beings in the process of remembering their truth.

That remembrance is powerful.

WE ARE BREAKING CYCLES OUR ANCESTORS NEVER HAD THE FREEDOM TO ADDRESS

For centuries, Black people had to suppress their emotional, mental, and spiritual needs simply to survive. Survival left no room for self-reflection, no space for healing, no bandwidth for vulnerability.

But now we do.

We are the first generation with the time, tools, and cultural permission to slow down long enough to ask:

"What hurt me?"
"What shaped me?"
"What am I carrying that isn't mine?"

"What do I need?"
"How do I heal?"

These questions are powerful, because healing begins with awareness.
And awareness leads to liberation.

We are doing the emotional and psychological work that our ancestors prayed for but never had the safety to pursue.

Breaking cycles requires courage that is often misunderstood. It is easier to carry inherited patterns than to confront them. It is easier to normalize pain than to question it. And yet, this generation is choosing the harder path.

We are choosing honesty.

Honesty about how trauma shaped behavior.
Honesty about how silence became survival.
Honesty about how strength sometimes masked suffering.

This honesty is not an indictment of our ancestors. It is an act of reverence. It honors their endurance by refusing to pass forward what they never had the chance to release.

This work is sacred.

By naming what was unnamed and feeling what was unfelt, we are completing cycles that began long before us. We are finishing emotional and spiritual work that was interrupted by necessity. In doing so, we are restoring continuity to our lineage.

Healing, in this sense, becomes an act of ancestral fulfillment.

THERAPY IS BECOMING A PATHWAY, NOT A TABOO

The stigma around mental health once kept our community in silence. But today, therapy has become:

- normalized
- accessible
- respected
- proactive
- integrated into daily life

Black therapists, counselors, coaches, and healers are creating culturally aligned spaces where vulnerability is a strength, not a liability.

We are learning to feel, express, process, and release.
We are learning language our grandparents didn't have access to:

- boundaries
- triggers
- self-care
- emotional regulation
- attachment styles
- trauma responses

Therapy is becoming a tool for freedom, not shame.
And freedom is contagious.

What is especially transformative about the rise of therapy is how it reframes self responsibility. Therapy is not about blame. It is about agency. It asks individuals to examine their inner world not to judge it, but to understand it.

Understanding creates choice.

When people understand their patterns, they can interrupt them. When they understand their triggers, they can respond rather than react. When they understand their needs, they can advocate for themselves without guilt.

This internal agency reduces dependency on external validation. People become less reactive to criticism and less controlled by fear. They make decisions from clarity rather than conditioning.

This is emotional sovereignty.

And sovereignty at the emotional level translates directly into leadership, creativity, and relational health.

SPIRITUAL AWAKENING IS EXPANDING BEYOND TRADITIONAL FRAMEWORKS

We are honoring our religious roots while expanding into a more personal, universal, and intuitive spirituality. Black people today are embracing:

- meditation
- ancestral veneration
- mindfulness
- metaphysics
- holistic healing
- breathwork
- Reiki and energy modalities
- spiritual psychology
- Divine intelligence
- inner child integration

This is not a rejection of God
it is a deeper connection to God.

We are discovering that spirituality is not found in fear, but in presence.
Not in punishment, but in love.
Not in conformity, but in awakening.

This spiritual expansion is lifting our consciousness, raising our vibration, and unlocking levels of creativity, clarity, and peace that previous generations could not access.

This expansion of spirituality also reflects a reclaiming of intuition as a legitimate form of intelligence. For generations, Black intuition was dismissed, feared, or labeled as irrational. Yet intuition has always been one of our most refined survival tools.

Now, it is becoming a tool for thriving.

By reconnecting with intuition, people are learning to trust their inner guidance. They are listening to their bodies. They are discerning alignment rather than chasing approval. This intuitive literacy supports decision making that is both practical and spiritually grounded.

It also reduces fragmentation.

When mind, body, and spirit are integrated, people experience coherence. This coherence stabilizes nervous systems, deepens presence, and expands creativity. Life begins to feel less like a series of reactions and more like a guided unfolding.

This is spiritual maturity.

WE ARE LEARNING TO PRIORITIZE WHOLENESS OVER HUSTLE

Black people have always been extraordinary at working hard.
But now, we are learning something revolutionary:

Healing is also productive.
Rest is also resistance.
Joy is also justice.
Peace is also power.

We are no longer defining success through burnout, sacrifice, or emotional suppression.
We are defining it through alignment, authenticity, and wellbeing.

This shift is reshaping:

- how we love
- how we parent
- how we lead
- how we create
- how we relate to ourselves
- how we navigate the world

Wholeness is becoming the new standard.

Prioritizing wholeness also dismantles one of the most harmful myths imposed on Black bodies, the belief that our worth is measured by productivity alone. This belief normalized exhaustion and framed rest as indulgence rather than necessity.

That myth is losing its grip.

As people reconnect with their humanity, they are redefining success in ways that honor sustainability. They are asking whether achievements are aligned with wellbeing. They are choosing paths that allow space for joy, connection, and presence.

This recalibration changes how time is valued.

Time becomes something to inhabit rather than consume. Moments are savored. Relationships are nurtured. Life is experienced more fully. This richness enhances creativity and resilience far more than constant striving ever could.

Wholeness is not a retreat from ambition. It is an expansion of it.

WE ARE RECLAIMING OUR INNER WORLD AS SACRED TERRITORY

For too long, Black inner life, our emotions, thoughts, and spiritual truths, has been overshadowed by external struggle. But this movement is bringing us back to the sacred truth:

Our inner world is where our power lives.

We are journaling, meditating, reflecting, praying, and practicing presence.
We are tending to our hearts, our nervous systems, our beliefs, our spirit, and our intuition.

This is more than self-care.
It is soul-care.
It is legacy work.
It is generational transformation.

When we heal ourselves, we heal our children.
When we elevate our consciousness, we elevate our future.

Treating the inner world as sacred also restores dignity. It affirms that emotions are not liabilities to suppress, but signals to interpret. That inner experiences deserve care, attention, and respect.

This dignity transforms self relationship.

People who honor their inner world set healthier boundaries. They recognize when something is misaligned. They trust themselves. This trust reduces dependence on external affirmation and increases inner stability.

Stability creates courage.

Courage allows people to speak truth, pursue purpose, and take risks aligned with their values. It allows them to leave environments that diminish them and invest in spaces that nourish them.

This internal strength radiates outward.

CLOSING: A HEALED PEOPLE CREATE A NEW WORLD

The mental, emotional, and spiritual transformation movement is not a trend, it is the rebirth of Black consciousness. It is preparing us for a future in which we lead not from our wounds, but from our wisdom. Not from our pain, but from our purpose. Not from trauma, but from truth.

This healing revolution is one of the clearest signs the future belongs to us
because a healed people think differently, love differently, create differently, and lead differently.

We are stepping into a new era of identity, grounded in:

clarity
peace
truth
alignment
purpose
joy
and Divine connection.

And from this place of inner power, there is nothing we cannot build.
Nothing we cannot transform.
Nothing we cannot become.

Perhaps the most profound implication of this transformation is that it restores hope without denial. It does not require forgetting the past. It does not ask for blind optimism. It is grounded hope, born from clarity rather than illusion.

This hope is resilient.

It can coexist with complexity. It can hold grief and joy at the same time. It understands that healing is not linear, but it trusts the direction of growth.

A people who trust their inner evolution are not easily discouraged.

They know that progress is unfolding even when it is not immediately visible. They understand that inner shifts precede outer change. And they move forward with patience and faith.

That faith is not passive.

It is active.
It is embodied.
It is creative.

And it is shaping the future now.

This is our awakening.
This is our evolution.
This is our moment.

And the future is calling.

And perhaps the most extraordinary dimension of this transformation movement is how deeply it is reshaping the relationship Black people have with our own inner lives. For the first time in our history on this soil, we are treating our minds, our emotions, and our spirits as sacred spaces rather than burdens to hide or battles to fight alone. We are no longer ashamed of our sensitivity, our vulnerability, or our complexity. Instead, we are embracing these aspects as signs of wisdom, not weakness.

This reclamation of inner space is radical.
It means we are learning to sit with ourselves rather than run from ourselves.
It means we are unlearning generational habits of emotional suppression.
It means we are releasing identities tied to struggle and choosing identities rooted in possibility.
It means we are allowing ourselves to *feel* in ways our ancestors could not safely feel.

This is liberation at the deepest level, liberation from the inside out.

You can see this liberation in the way Black people are talking to each other. Conversations once dominated by survival, stress, and frustration now include questions like:

"How's your heart?"
"What are you healing from?"
"What brings you peace?"
"What are you learning about yourself?"
"What are you letting go of?"
"What is your spirit saying?"

These questions signal a cultural maturity — a shift away from viewing emotional life as dangerous and toward seeing it as divine. And when a people begin to engage with their inner world from a place of empowerment, they unlock capacities that generations of oppression attempted to bury.

This is why creativity is exploding.
This is why entrepreneurship is expanding.
This is why leadership is evolving.
This is why relationships are deepening.
This is why community is strengthening.

Healing is not just something that happens in therapy, it is something that spills into every corner of life.

Another extraordinary dimension of this movement is the rise of Black healers, therapists, coaches, spiritual teachers, wellness practitioners, and consciousness leaders. These individuals are not only guiding others, they are reimagining what healing looks like for our community. They are blending psychology with spirituality, ancestral wisdom with modern science, emotional literacy with cultural understanding. They are creating frameworks of wellbeing that center Black identity rather than erase it.

For the first time, Black people can heal in spaces where they are fully seen.
Fully valued.
Fully affirmed.
Fully understood.

This is healing without translation.
Healing without shrinking.
Healing without code-switching.
Healing without apology.

And the ripple effects are generational.

Children raised by healed parents inherit less trauma and more emotional intelligence.
Families shaped by healing create cycles of love instead of cycles of silence.
Communities shaped by healing develop resilience without hardness.
Leaders shaped by healing bring empathy to power.
Creators shaped by healing produce art that liberates rather than retraumatizes.

The entire ecosystem of Black life is being renewed through this movement.

And perhaps the most important truth of all is this:
Healing expands imagination.
A healed mind can dream bigger.
A healed heart can love deeper.
A healed spirit can rise higher.

This is why the future belongs to us
because we are releasing what once bound us,
remembering who we truly are,
and awakening to everything we are meant to become.

A healed people also communicate differently. Conversations shift from blame to curiosity. From accusation to understanding. From silence to honesty. This shift reduces internal conflict and strengthens collective cohesion.

Cohesion amplifies impact.

When people are emotionally regulated, they collaborate more effectively. They listen more deeply. They resolve conflict with intention rather than escalation. This emotional intelligence becomes a cultural asset.

It influences how movements are built, how institutions are led, and how communities respond to challenge.

Healing, then, is not private. It is strategic.

"Still I rise."

— **Maya Angelou**

CHAPTER 20

OUR RESILIENCE IS OUR SUPERPOWER

Why Our History Proves We Are Built for the Future

If there is one defining trait that has carried Black people through centuries of oppression, displacement, violence, injustice, and systemic sabotage, it is resilience. Not the shallow, survival-based resilience society romanticizes, but the deep, soul-level resilience that transforms wounds into wisdom, pressure into purpose, and adversity into evolution.

Our resilience is not accidental.
It is ancestral.
It is encoded in our DNA.
It is woven into our history.
It is carried in our spirit.
It is the fuel that has powered every step of our journey on this soil.

And today, as we stand on the threshold of a new future, our resilience is not just a reminder of what we've survived —
it is evidence that we are built for what comes next.

What is often overlooked in conversations about resilience is that it is not merely a reaction to harm. It is a form of intelligence. It reflects an ability to assess conditions, adapt strategies, and preserve essence even when circumstances attempt to erase it.

This intelligence operates on multiple levels at once.

It shows up emotionally, in the capacity to feel deeply without being destroyed by feeling. It shows up psychologically, in the ability to reinterpret experience rather than internalize oppression as identity. It shows up spiritually, in the refusal to surrender meaning even when systems deny worth.

Resilience, in this sense, is not passive endurance. It is active orientation. It is the capacity to remain in relationship with life even when life has been hostile.

That orientation is what allows evolution to continue.

What makes this resilience so extraordinary is that it has never been dependent on favorable conditions. It was forged in environments designed to deny dignity, distort identity, and suppress possibility. And yet, even under those conditions, Black people continued to imagine, create, and love.

Imagination itself became an act of resistance.

To imagine freedom while enslaved, to imagine joy while oppressed, to imagine wholeness while fractured by systems, required a depth of inner strength that cannot be measured by conventional standards. This imaginative resilience allowed Black people to live inwardly expansive lives even when outward circumstances were constricted.

That inner expansion laid the groundwork for every outward breakthrough that followed.

WE HAVE ENDURED WHAT SHOULD HAVE BROKEN US — YET WE RISE

No other group in American history has endured the depth, scale, and duration of systemic oppression that Black people have. And yet, despite everything designed to break us, we stand today not merely alive, but evolving.

We survived:

- enslavement
- family separation

- cultural erasure
- economic exclusion
- Jim Crow
- redlining
- mass incarceration
- discriminatory education
- political disenfranchisement
- medical neglect
- propaganda and stereotypes

The fact that we not only survived but *thrived* in spite of this is not a coincidence — it is a testament to our spiritual fortitude.

Our story is not one of defeat.
Our story is one of divine endurance.

Endurance at this scale produces more than survival. It produces insight. Black resilience carries a level of emotional intelligence that comes from navigating complexity for generations. It has sharpened our ability to read environments, adapt to shifting dynamics, and respond creatively under pressure.

This intelligence is not accidental.

It is the result of continuous problem solving in hostile conditions. It is the reason Black innovation so often emerges at the intersection of necessity and creativity. When resources were scarce, ingenuity filled the gap. When opportunity was denied, alternatives were created.

This adaptive intelligence is now one of our greatest assets in a rapidly changing world.

As societies face uncertainty, disruption, and transformation, the skills honed through Black resilience are becoming universally relevant. Flexibility, creativity, emotional regulation, and community orientation are no longer optional traits. They are essential.

Survival at this scale requires more than strength. It requires coherence. It requires the ability to maintain a sense of self across fragmentation, loss, and interruption. Black communities preserved coherence through story, ritual, music, humor, spirituality, and shared memory.

These were not luxuries. They were technologies.

They allowed people to remember who they were even when identity was under assault. They allowed values to persist even when institutions were hostile. They allowed hope to circulate even when evidence was scarce.

This coherence explains why Black culture remained alive rather than fossilized. It evolved because it was relational rather than rigid. It adapted without losing its core.

That capacity to evolve without erasing self is one of the most sophisticated forms of resilience a people can possess.

RESILIENCE DOES NOT MEAN WE ACCEPT SUFFERING — IT MEANS WE OUTGROW IT

One of the most misunderstood aspects of Black resilience is the assumption that it means we are willing to tolerate pain indefinitely. But true resilience is not about enduring suffering — it is about transcending it.

We have learned to:

- adapt
- innovate
- reinvent
- transform

- rebuild
- heal
- rise

Resilience is not our trauma response —
it is our evolutionary advantage.

It means we know how to create without permission.
It means we know how to build from nothing.
It means we know how to rise after every fall.

This capacity to convert adversity into advancement is one of the reasons our future is so powerful.

Outgrowing suffering also requires discernment. It means recognizing when endurance has served its purpose and when it has become a barrier to evolution. For generations, endurance was necessary. It was a means of survival in environments that offered little protection.

But endurance without healing carries a cost.

Today, resilience is being redefined to include discernment, self protection, and intentional release. Black people are learning that strength does not require perpetual sacrifice. Growth does not require self abandonment. Love does not require suffering.

This reframing allows resilience to evolve from reaction to wisdom.

Wisdom knows when to push and when to pause. Wisdom knows when to persist and when to pivot. Wisdom understands that rest is not weakness, but restoration.

This evolved resilience is lighter. It carries less weight. And because of that, it moves faster and further.

Outgrowing suffering also involves redefining loyalty. For generations, loyalty was often confused with endurance. Staying meant strength. Leaving meant failure. Questioning meant betrayal.

Those definitions are changing.

Today, resilience includes the courage to walk away from what diminishes the soul. It includes the wisdom to recognize when endurance is no longer virtuous, but harmful. It includes permission to choose peace without guilt.

This evolution does not dishonor the past. It completes it.

By releasing what no longer serves growth, Black people are honoring the original purpose of resilience, which was never to suffer endlessly, but to survive long enough to reach freedom.

Freedom includes emotional freedom.

And emotional freedom expands possibility.

WE TURN EVERY SYSTEM THAT EXCLUDED US INTO A SYSTEM WE TRANSFORM

History shows a pattern:
Every system that tried to exclude us eventually became a system we reshaped.

Music?
We created genres the world still imitates.

Sports?
We redefined dominance.

Art?
We revolutionized expression.

Entrepreneurship?
We are building global empires.

Politics?
We are influencing national elections.

Education?
We are redefining the pathways to knowledge.

Healing?
We are leading the wellness movement.

Creativity, culture, innovation — every time the world tried to reduce us, we expanded. Every time it tried to silence us, we amplified. Every time it put limits on us, we broke them.

That is resilience.

Transformation at this level reveals something essential about Black resilience. It is not oppositional by nature. It is creative. It does not simply resist systems. It reimagines them.

Rather than seeking inclusion within broken frameworks, Black communities have consistently built parallel systems rooted in dignity, innovation, and care. These systems were not designed to replicate exclusion, but to correct it.

This pattern reflects a deep understanding of power.

True power does not require domination. It requires creation. It requires the ability to envision alternatives and bring them into existence. Black resilience has always been aligned with this creative power.

And now, as access expands, this creative instinct is being applied on a global scale.

Transformation at this level requires imagination paired with courage. It requires the willingness to envision alternatives when none appear obvious. Black resilience has always been visionary.

Vision preceded infrastructure.

Before schools existed, learning was passed orally. Before ownership was permitted, economies were created within community. Before political access was granted, leadership was practiced informally. These parallel systems were not temporary fixes. They were rehearsals for future sovereignty.

Now, as access expands, those rehearsed skills are being applied at scale.

What once sustained survival is now fueling innovation. What once preserved dignity is now generating influence. This continuity explains why Black leadership often feels intuitive rather than learned. It has been practiced for generations under different names.

OUR JOY IS PROOF OF OUR STRENGTH

Perhaps the most profound expression of Black resilience is our joy — vibrant, expressive, expansive, contagious joy. Joy that exists not because life has been easy, but because our spirit refuses to be crushed.

Our joy is medicine.
Our laughter is rebellion.
Our creativity is liberation.
Our love is endurance.
Our community is strength.

Joy is not a trivial part of our culture —
it is a survival technology.

And it is one of the clearest indicators that we are built for the future.

Joy as survival technology deserves deeper recognition. Joy regulated nervous systems when safety was not guaranteed. It preserved humanity in conditions that attempted to strip it away. It reminded people of who they were beyond what was imposed upon them.

Joy was not denial.

It was defiance.

By choosing joy, Black people refused to let suffering define the entirety of their existence. They asserted presence, connection, and aliveness in the face of dehumanization. That assertion preserved identity across generations.

Today, joy continues to function as a stabilizing force. It grounds people in the present. It builds community. It restores balance. And it fuels creativity that is essential for future building.

Joy also serves as a corrective to despair. Despair narrows vision. It convinces people that the present is permanent and the future is closed. Joy interrupts that narrative.

It reminds the body that aliveness is possible now, not someday.

This embodied reminder matters. When people experience joy, even briefly, their nervous systems regulate. Their perspective widens. Creativity returns. Possibility reenters the conversation.

This is why joy has always been communal in Black culture. It is shared because it is sustaining. It lifts not just individuals, but environments.

Joy, then, is not escapism. It is grounding. It anchors people in the present while keeping them oriented toward the future.

WE CARRY THE WISDOM OF GENERATIONS AND THE COURAGE OF THE PRESENT

Black resilience is not just historical — it is generational.
Our ancestors endured the unimaginable so we could imagine the impossible.
They survived so we could thrive.
They prayed so we could manifest.
They held on so we could let go.
They walked so we could soar.

Today, we carry their wisdom in our blood and their courage in our bones.
This heritage gives us a spiritual advantage — a knowing that we have already overcome more than most humans will ever comprehend.

Because of that, the challenges of the future cannot intimidate us.

We are built for complexity.
We are built for change.
We are built for innovation.
We are built for healing.
We are built for possibility.
We are built for leadership.
We are built for greatness.

Resilience is not just what we have —
it is who we are.

Identity rooted in resilience does not mean identity rooted in struggle. It means identity rooted in capacity. Capacity to respond. Capacity to adapt. Capacity to transform.

This distinction matters because it shifts self perception.

When people see themselves as capable rather than wounded, they approach life differently. They take risks. They imagine futures. They invest in long term goals. They trust their ability to navigate uncertainty.

This trust reduces fear and increases agency.

Agency is the bridge between history and future.

Generational wisdom is not static knowledge. It is lived understanding. It includes emotional patterns, relational strategies, spiritual practices, and survival insights passed down through story, behavior, and belief.

This wisdom lives in the body.

It informs instinct. It shapes response. It guides intuition. And when combined with modern awareness and healing, it becomes a powerful compass for navigating complexity.

Black people are now integrating ancestral wisdom with contemporary tools, psychology, and spirituality. This integration allows the past to inform the future without constraining it.

It creates continuity without confinement.

Carrying generational wisdom also requires discernment about what to keep and what to release. Not every inherited pattern is meant to continue. Some were adaptive responses to specific conditions that no longer exist.

Resilience includes the ability to update.

This updating process is underway as Black communities reevaluate beliefs around masculinity, femininity, success, rest, vulnerability, and worth. These reevaluations are not signs of weakness. They are signs of confidence.

A people unsure of themselves cling to tradition rigidly. A people secure in their identity refine tradition thoughtfully.

This refinement ensures that wisdom remains alive rather than becoming a burden.

CLOSING: THE FUTURE FAVORS THOSE WHO KNOW HOW TO RISE

The future belongs to us not because the past was easy, but because the past prepared us.
Our history is not a weight — it is training.
It is not a burden — it is a blueprint.
It is not a curse — it is a calling.

We have inherited the strongest foundation any people could ever ask for:
the ability to rise, again and again, without losing our humanity.

This resilience is our superpower —
a force the world has underestimated for centuries,
and a force that will shape the next era of Black evolution.

We have risen before.
We are rising now.
And we will continue to rise into a future that was always meant for us.

Understanding resilience as transmutation reframes adversity entirely. Adversity becomes raw material rather than destiny. It becomes information rather than identity.

This reframing does not minimize harm. It contextualizes it.

By seeing adversity as something that can be worked with rather than something that defines worth, people reclaim authorship over their lives. They choose how experience is metabolized. They decide what meaning is extracted.

This authorship is liberating.

It allows people to honor pain without centering it. It allows gratitude to coexist with grief. It allows growth to occur without erasure of history.

And yet, even as we honor our resilience, we must also understand its deeper meaning. Our resilience is not simply about survival — it is about *transmutation.* It is the ability to take the harshest ingredients life has offered us and alchemize them into wisdom, empathy, creativity, brilliance, and innovation. This is not the resilience of brute endurance — it is the resilience of the soul, the resilience of transformation, the resilience of a people who know how to turn every wound into a window and every barrier into a breakthrough.

Resilience is not what kept us alive —
it is what kept us *becoming.*

We became artists when we were denied literacy.
We became innovators when we were denied resources.
We became healers when we were denied care.
We became leaders when we were denied agency.
We became creators when we were denied access.

At every turn, when the world attempted to restrict our evolution, we simply changed form and evolved anyway.

This ability to reinvent ourselves in the face of adversity is not something that can be taught in schools or learned from books. It is ancestral memory. It is spiritual inheritance. It is the quiet, powerful, unbreakable thread that connects us to those who came before us.

And what makes this resilience even more powerful today is that we are finally learning to pair it with healing. For generations, resilience meant enduring without breaking — but now, resilience means thriving without carrying unnecessary weight. It means acknowledging the wounds without becoming them. It means releasing the emotional burdens our ancestors never had the freedom to let go of. It means redefining what strength looks like.

Strength no longer means silence.
Strength no longer means suppression.
Strength no longer means ignoring our needs.
Strength no longer means performing perfection.

Strength now means wholeness.
Strength means self-awareness.
Strength means emotional literacy.
Strength means softness when softness is needed.
Strength means boundaries.
Strength means rest.
Strength means joy.

This shift is revolutionary — because when a people learn to pair resilience with healing, their power becomes exponential.

We are no longer just surviving systems —
we are outgrowing them.

We are no longer just responding to the world —
we are reshaping it.

We are no longer defined by what happened to us —
we are defined by what we are becoming.

And what we are becoming is extraordinary.

You can see this evolution in the dreams of young Black people who no longer measure themselves against the limits of the past. You can see it in the confidence of Black creators who no longer wait for gatekeepers. You can see it in the assertiveness of Black leaders who no longer shrink in the face of opposition. You can see it in the emotional maturity of Black families who are breaking generational cycles. You can see it in the spiritual awakening of Black communities who are reconnecting with ancient wisdom.

Our resilience is no longer reactive.
It is generative.
It is intentional.
It is expansive.
It is future-focused.

This is why the future belongs to us —
because we have already proven, time and time again, that there is nothing we cannot rise from, nothing we cannot transform, nothing we cannot build, and nothing we cannot become.

Our resilience is not merely a response to our history —
it is the technology of our becoming.

The convergence of resilience and wholeness represents a turning point. Resilience alone ensured survival. Wholeness ensures sustainability.

When people are whole, they are less reactive. They are more intentional. They are capable of building without reproducing harm. This integration changes not only outcomes, but the quality of the journey.

It allows progress without burnout. Growth without fragmentation. Power without loss of humanity.

This is the evolution now underway.

The meeting of resilience and wholeness is not an endpoint. It is a beginning. It signals a transition from reactive evolution to conscious creation.

When people are whole, they build differently. They do not replicate harm unconsciously. They do not confuse control with leadership. They do not mistake endurance for destiny.

They create systems aligned with dignity.

This alignment will shape everything that follows.

And the world has not yet seen what happens when Black resilience meets Black wholeness, Black imagination, and Black unity.

But it is about to.

Rising also requires vision. It requires the ability to see beyond immediate conditions and imagine what does not yet exist. Black resilience has always included this visionary capacity.

Vision sustained hope when evidence was scarce.

That same vision is now being applied to future building. Black communities are envisioning systems rooted in equity, wellness, creativity, and shared prosperity. They are not waiting for permission to imagine better futures. They are actively designing them.

This proactive stance transforms resilience into leadership.

"The time is always right to do what is right."

— **Dr. Martin Luther King Jr.**

CHAPTER 21

THE CHOICE BEFORE US

Stepping Into Agency, Responsibility, and Collective Possibility

Every generation reaches a crossroads — a moment when the past and the future stand side by side, waiting for a decision. Not a decision made by institutions, politicians, or systems, but a decision made within the hearts and minds of everyday people. For Black America, that moment is now.

We are standing in a rare space where our past no longer dictates our destiny, and our future has never looked more expansive, more promising, or more within reach. We have more knowledge, more visibility, more autonomy, more creativity, more connectivity, and more opportunity than at any time since our arrival in this country.

But opportunity alone does not create transformation.
Transformation requires choice.

Choice is the doorway between awareness and action. Awareness alone can inspire, but without choice it remains theoretical. Choice is what turns insight into movement and possibility into reality.

For Black America, this distinction is critical.

We have always possessed awareness. Awareness of injustice. Awareness of inequality. Awareness of our own brilliance. What is different now is that awareness is no longer paired primarily with reaction. It is being paired with intention.

Intention introduces agency.

Agency means recognizing that while we did not choose the conditions that shaped our past, we do choose how those conditions shape our future. It means understanding that power is not only something that operates upon us, but something that flows through us.

When a people step into agency, they stop asking what is allowed and start asking what is aligned. That shift changes everything.

The choice to rise beyond old narratives.
The choice to release limiting beliefs.
The choice to heal instead of perpetuate harm.
The choice to build instead of beg.
The choice to lead instead of wait.
The choice to imagine boldly instead of fearfully.
The choice to embody the future rather than inherit the past.

The question before us is not, *"Can we rise?"*
History has already answered that.
The real question is:
"Will we intentionally choose to step into our power?"

WE ARE NO LONGER DEFINED BY THE SYSTEMS THAT SHAPED OUR PAIN

For generations, Black life in America was shaped by systems that restricted our voice, our power, and our possibility. Those systems created the illusion that our greatest battles were external — racism, discrimination, exclusion, poverty, injustice. And while those forces still exist, something fundamental has shifted:

We now understand that the most transformative battles are internal.

The battle for identity.
The battle for self-worth.
The battle for consciousness.
The battle for healing.
The battle for purpose.
The battle for agency.

We are no longer trying to escape the systems that built our
oppression —
we are outgrowing them.
We are no longer defined by the trauma we inherited —
we are redefining ourselves through healing.
We are no longer shaped by what was taken —
we are expanding based on what is possible.

This is the moment where the inner world becomes the catalyst for
outer revolution.

Revolutions that begin externally often collapse under their own
weight. Revolutions that begin internally tend to endure. This is
because inner transformation changes behavior at its source.

When consciousness shifts, choices shift.
When choices shift, habits shift.
When habits shift, culture shifts.

This sequence is natural and unstoppable.

Black America is currently undergoing this kind of inner revolution.
It is visible in the questions being asked, the boundaries being set,
and the values being prioritized. People are choosing alignment over
approval. Healing over heroics. Purpose over performance.

These choices may appear subtle, but they are seismic.

They are reshaping families, redefining leadership, and reimagining
what success looks like across generations.

Outgrowing systems does not mean pretending they never existed.
It means refusing to let them remain the primary reference point for
identity. When systems shape pain, they often leave behind internal
echoes that persist long after external conditions change.

Those echoes sound like self doubt.
They sound like lowered expectations.
They sound like fear disguised as realism.

Choosing the future requires recognizing these internal residues and releasing them consciously. This is not denial. It is discernment.

Discernment allows us to separate what happened to us from who we are. It allows us to honor history without living inside it. And it restores authorship over our inner narrative.

This inner liberation is the foundation of all lasting change.

THE FUTURE WILL NOT BE BUILT BY CIRCUMSTANCE — IT WILL BE BUILT BY INTENTION

It is tempting to believe that progress is inevitable, that time alone will heal the wounds of history. But progress is not automatic; it is created through intentional action. It requires a collective decision to:

- elevate our consciousness
- take responsibility for our choices
- cultivate emotional maturity
- strengthen our communities
- support one another's visions
- build systems that reflect our values
- imagine futures beyond the limits of our past

Intention is the architect of destiny.

And the beauty of this moment is that Black America is becoming more intentional than ever before — about healing, parenting, relationships, creativity, entrepreneurship, spirituality, and leadership.

Intentionality also demands responsibility. Responsibility not as blame, but as authorship. It means recognizing that while systems influence outcomes, they do not dictate consciousness.

Responsibility asks us to examine how we participate in the narratives we inherit. Which stories do we repeat without questioning? Which beliefs do we protect even when they limit us? Which fears do we normalize instead of challenging?

This level of responsibility is empowering.

It returns control to the individual and the collective. It affirms that change is not something we wait for, but something we practice daily through choices large and small.

We are choosing growth.
We are choosing alignment.
We are choosing evolution.
We are choosing possibility.

Intention is not wishful thinking. It is disciplined clarity. It requires attention, responsibility, and follow through. When a people become intentional, they stop drifting between inherited scripts and start designing new ones.

Design requires vision.

Vision allows us to ask not just what we want to escape, but what we want to create. It moves the conversation beyond survival and into architecture. What kind of communities do we want to live in? What kind of relationships do we want to model? What kind of legacy do we want to leave?

These questions are now being asked widely across Black America.

And questions shape futures.

THE INTERNAL SHIFT WILL SHAPE THE EXTERNAL WORLD

The greatest civil rights movement of this century will not take place in the streets — it will take place in our hearts, minds, and homes. It will be expressed through:

- healed families
- emotionally intelligent men

- empowered women

- inspired youth

- conscious elders

- spiritually grounded communities

- purpose-driven leadership

- creative entrepreneurs

- unified networks

- global connection

When the inner world changes, the outer world has no choice but to follow.

This is why the choice before us is so powerful —
because the world cannot transform into something we have not first become.

External change without internal alignment often recreates old patterns in new forms. History has shown this repeatedly. New leaders emerge, but old dynamics persist. New opportunities arise, but familiar limitations follow.

Internal alignment interrupts this cycle.

When values are clarified internally, systems built externally reflect those values. Leadership becomes service rather than dominance. Wealth becomes circulation rather than accumulation. Power becomes stewardship rather than control.

This alignment is what allows progress to be sustainable rather than temporary.

WE ARE BEING ASKED TO CHOOSE OUR HIGHEST FUTURE

The universe has placed a series of doors before Black America. Each door represents a different level of consciousness, opportunity, and identity. Behind one door is more of the same — old patterns, old fears, old stories. Behind another is incremental progress. But behind the third door — the door we are being called toward — is a future rooted in empowerment, agency, unity, creativity, abundance, and spiritual awakening.

Choosing this future does not require perfection.
It requires willingness.
Willingness to expand.
Willingness to evolve.
Willingness to see ourselves differently.
Willingness to imagine without limits.
Willingness to take responsibility for the life we are creating.

The next era of Black evolution will not be determined by oppression.
It will be determined by choice.

Being asked implies readiness. Life does not ask questions we are not prepared to answer. The invitation before Black America exists because the capacity to respond has already developed.

Capacity built through resilience.
Through adaptation.
Through creativity.
Through survival.

Now that capacity is being redirected toward creation.

Choosing a higher future does not mean abandoning realism. It means expanding realism to include possibility. It means understanding that what has never been done before still exists within the realm of the possible.

Every breakthrough in history began as an act of imagination before it became an act of execution.

CLOSING: THE CHOICE BEFORE US IS AN INVITATION — NOT A THREAT

This moment is not asking us to fix everything at once.
It is asking us to turn inward and upward.
To choose healing over hurt.
To choose vision over fear.
To choose abundance over scarcity.
To choose unity over fragmentation.
To choose agency over victimhood.
To choose the future over the past.

The choice before us is simple:
Do we step into the fullness of who we are —
or do we dim our own light?

Do we build the world our ancestors dreamed of —
or do we settle for inherited limitations?

Do we rise —
or do we remain?

Everything we need is already within us.
Everything we desire is already calling us.
Everything we imagine is already available.

The future belongs to us…
but only if we choose it.

And yet, as powerful as this collective moment is, the truth is that no
transformation happens by accident.
Every breakthrough begins with a decision.
Every revolution begins with a shift in consciousness.
Every movement forward begins with a moment of clarity in which
a people choose — often quietly, often internally — to no longer
live inside a story that was never designed for them.

We are in that moment.

This is the moment when the residue of old conditioning becomes visible enough for us to release.
This is the moment when inherited narratives feel too small to contain our expanding identity.
This is the moment when we begin questioning not the world outside us, but the world within us.
This is the moment when we begin to understand that change is not something that happens *to* a people — it is something that happens *through* a people.

The choice before us is not simply about the direction of Black America —
it is about the direction of Black consciousness.

Do we continue to define ourselves through a lens of struggle?
Or do we step into a narrative of possibility?

Do we see our trauma as identity?
Or do we treat it as the soil from which a wiser version of ourselves can grow?

Do we allow outdated systems to determine our worth?
Or do we become the architects of new systems that reflect our brilliance?

Do we accept the limiting beliefs passed down through generations?
Or do we become the generation that ends cycles rather than inherits them?

These are spiritual questions.
Evolutionary questions.
Questions only a conscious people can answer.

And Black America is becoming deeply, profoundly conscious.

This consciousness is visible in the way we parent, the way we love, the way we heal, the way we speak truth, the way we pursue purpose, the way we build community, the way we create art, and the way we imagine our place in the world. We are no longer waiting for outside forces to grant us permission; we are granting it to ourselves.

We must also recognize that choosing our future does not require collective agreement — it requires collective momentum.
Movements are not built on perfection or unanimity.
They are built on energy, vision, and alignment.

If enough of us choose healing…
healing becomes culture.

If enough of us choose purpose…
purpose becomes direction.

If enough of us choose unity…
unity becomes identity.

If enough of us choose possibility…
possibility becomes destiny.

And we are already seeing these shifts everywhere — in art, entrepreneurship, spirituality, activism, mental health, tech, creativity, education, community-building, and global connectivity. We are choosing, even when we do not realize it, a different version of ourselves.

This is how futures are born.

Not through speeches or declarations, but through quiet, steady, collective choices that reshape the arc of a people's evolution.
And at this very moment, Black America is making choices that align with liberation, expansion, and self-determination.

The choice before us is not a burden —
it is a blessing.
It is a sacred invitation.
It is an open door to a future worthy of our lineage and worthy of our dreams.

We stand on the edge of possibility with everything we need to walk through the doorway.

Our ancestors endured unimaginable hardship so that we could stand here with this freedom, this awareness, this clarity, this agency.
The only question now is:
Will we honor their sacrifice by choosing the future they believed we deserved?

Choosing the future is not a single act. It is a practice. It is renewed daily through thought, behavior, relationship, and intention.

Some days the choice will be clear.
Some days it will feel difficult.
Some days it will require courage.

But each choice reinforces the next.

Over time, these choices create momentum. Momentum creates culture. Culture shapes destiny.

And destiny, once chosen consciously, becomes inevitable.

The future belongs to us —
but only if we consciously, courageously, unapologetically choose it.

Invitations honor free will. They do not coerce. They do not shame. They simply present an opening and wait for a response.

This moment is doing the same.

It is not demanding that Black America become something else. It is inviting us to become more fully who we already are. To step into dimensions of ourselves that were once suppressed or deferred.

The invitation is gentle, but its implications are vast.

"We were never meant just to survive."

— Audre Lorde
(A reminder that our existence itself is revolutionary.)

CHAPTER 22

A VISION FOR THE NEXT 100 YEARS

What a Fully Empowered Black America
Can Become

If you want to measure the strength of a people, look not at what they have survived, but at what they are capable of becoming. For Black America, the next 100 years represent the most extraordinary evolutionary opportunity in our history. Not because the world will suddenly hand us equality, and not because oppressive systems will magically disappear — but because *we are becoming the kind of people who no longer depend on those systems to define what is possible.*

This chapter is not a prediction.
It is an invitation.
It is a vision of what Black America can become when we align
our consciousness, our creativity, our unity, and our spiritual power
toward shaping our collective destiny.

For the first time, we have the tools, the wisdom, the connectivity, and the freedom to design our future with intention rather than reaction.

The next 100 years are not something we hope for.
They are something we build.

Building implies participation. It requires engagement rather than observation. Futures are not constructed by spectators, but by contributors who understand that even small choices ripple forward across generations.

This realization reframes responsibility.

Responsibility becomes less about burden and more about opportunity. Each decision, each belief, each value we embody becomes a brick in the structure future generations will inhabit. This is why consciousness matters so deeply. Conscious builders create environments that sustain life. Unconscious builders often recreate harm without intention.

The future is asking for conscious architects.

And Black America is uniquely prepared for this role because we understand what it means to survive poorly designed systems. That lived knowledge becomes wisdom when applied intentionally. It allows us to build structures rooted in dignity, equity, and humanity rather than control or extraction.

THE FIRST PILLAR: A GENERATION OF HEALED AND CONSCIOUS BLACK YOUTH

Imagine Black children growing up emotionally literate, spiritually grounded, culturally confident, and fully aware of their brilliance. Imagine a generation raised without internalized inferiority — children who never have to recover from the wounds we inherited.

In this future:

- therapy is normalized from childhood
- mindfulness is part of education
- SEL is integrated into Black households
- emotional regulation is taught like mathematics
- authenticity is celebrated
- creativity is encouraged
- identity is affirmed

A generation that begins life healed will build a world we cannot yet imagine.

A healed generation also changes how adulthood unfolds. When children grow up emotionally supported rather than emotionally suppressed, they enter adulthood with resilience rather than repair work. They are not consumed by unlearning harm. They are free to focus on creation.

This freedom is revolutionary.

It allows young adults to invest energy in innovation rather than recovery. It reduces cycles of dysfunction. It strengthens relationships. It supports healthier parenting in the next generation. Healing compounds across time.

This is how generational transformation accelerates.

When healing begins early, progress does not move in slow increments. It leaps.

THE SECOND PILLAR: A COMPLETE REIMAGINING OF BLACK EDUCATION

In the next century, education becomes a liberation tool, not a sorting system. HBCUs are thriving epicenters of innovation. Black-owned digital learning platforms rival major universities. Community-based academies combine technology, culture, and mentorship. Children learn African history alongside STEM. Spiritual development is treated as foundational education.

Education becomes:

- personalized
- culturally grounded
- technologically empowered
- community-supported
- globally connected
- joy-centered

Knowledge becomes the great equalizer — not because society changed, but because *we changed society.*

Education that liberates does more than transfer information. It shapes identity. When learners see themselves reflected in what they study, curiosity deepens. Confidence grows. Learning becomes relational rather than transactional.

This approach produces thinkers rather than test takers.

Thinkers ask better questions. They challenge assumptions. They innovate rather than replicate. In a future defined by complexity, this capacity will matter more than memorization or compliance.

By reimagining education, Black America is preparing not just students, but architects of new systems. People capable of designing solutions rather than navigating limitations.

THE THIRD PILLAR: A BLACK ECONOMIC RENAISSANCE

Over the next 100 years, Black America can build economic ecosystems that uplift entire communities rather than isolated individuals. We can create:

- Black venture capital networks
- Black cooperative economics models
- global diaspora investment groups
- Black-owned banks with digital reach
- real estate development collectives
- entrepreneurship pipelines for youth
- generational wealth systems

This is not fantasy — it is infrastructure.
And we are already building it.

Money becomes not a source of stress, but a source of empowerment. Wealth becomes not an exception, but a norm.

Economic ecosystems rooted in community also stabilize families. When wealth circulates locally, stress decreases. Opportunity expands. Young people see tangible examples of possibility.

This visibility matters.

When children grow up seeing entrepreneurship, ownership, and cooperation as normal, their sense of what is achievable expands naturally. Aspiration becomes embodied rather than abstract.

Economic health supports emotional health.

And emotional health fuels creativity, leadership, and resilience. These systems reinforce one another. That reinforcement is how sustainable prosperity is built.

THE FOURTH PILLAR: BLACK LEADERSHIP ROOTED IN CONSCIOUSNESS

Leadership in the next century will not be defined by titles, politics, or power — but by consciousness, empathy, emotional intelligence, and spiritual grounding.

Imagine Black leaders who:

- lead from healed identity
- govern with compassion
- understand trauma
- design policy through wellness
- operate from purpose rather than ego
- build community rather than division

This new leadership model will influence not just Black America,
but the entire world.
Humanity evolves when leadership evolves — and Black leadership
is evolving fast.

Conscious leadership also changes how power is experienced by those being led. It reduces fear. It increases trust. It creates environments where people feel valued rather than managed.

Trust accelerates collaboration.

When people trust leadership, they invest more fully. They contribute ideas. They take responsibility. They act with integrity even when unobserved. This collective engagement multiplies impact far beyond what any single leader could achieve.

This is leadership as stewardship.

And stewardship creates legacies that endure beyond individual lifetimes.

THE FIFTH PILLAR: GLOBAL BLACK UNITY ACROSS THE DIASPORA

In the next 100 years, the African diaspora becomes a global alliance — culturally, economically, spiritually, and strategically interconnected.

We will see:

- cross-continental business partnerships
- shared cultural celebrations
- global learning exchanges
- tech collaborations
- pan-African digital platforms
- diaspora travel networks
- economic treaties between Black nations
- united global advocacy

The diaspora becomes an economic and cultural superpower — not through domination, but through connection.

Global unity also expands perspective. When Black communities connect across borders, they exchange strategies, insights, and solutions. They learn from one another's successes and challenges.

This exchange strengthens resilience.

It reduces isolation. It broadens imagination. It reveals patterns that might otherwise remain invisible. Shared learning accelerates collective intelligence.

In an interconnected world, this kind of unity becomes a strategic advantage.

THE SIXTH PILLAR: BLACK CREATIVITY AS A GLOBAL CULTURAL ENGINE

The future of global culture will continue to be shaped by Black imagination — our music, our style, our stories, our spiritual energy, our innovation.

But in the next 100 years, ownership becomes the rule, not the exception. Our children will grow up learning:

"You don't just create culture — you own it."

Art becomes asset.
Stories become structure.
Creativity becomes capital.

And Black culture remains the heartbeat of the world.

Ownership of creativity also restores dignity. It affirms that imagination is not merely expressive, but generative. It produces value. It shapes systems. It builds futures.

When creators own their work, they retain narrative authority.

This authority protects authenticity. It ensures that culture evolves from within rather than being extracted or distorted. It allows creativity to remain aligned with community rather than detached from it.

Creative sovereignty strengthens cultural longevity.

THE SEVENTH PILLAR: A SPIRITUALLY AWAKENED BLACK AMERICA

The future will not only be built by our hands, but by our consciousness.

Imagine a community that embraces:

- meditation
- intuition
- ancestral wisdom
- spiritual sovereignty
- metaphysical insight
- universal connection
- Divine intelligence within

This spiritual awakening becomes our guiding compass.
A people connected to Source cannot be controlled by systems.
A people aligned with purpose cannot be manipulated by fear.

Spiritual awakening also provides grounding during uncertainty. When people are connected to something larger than circumstance, fear loses its grip. Decisions are made from alignment rather than anxiety.

This grounding stabilizes vision.

It allows communities to move forward with patience rather than panic. It supports long term thinking. It nurtures compassion even during conflict.

Spiritual grounding is not passive. It is clarifying.

CLOSING: THE NEXT 100 YEARS ARE OURS TO SHAPE

This vision is not utopian.
It is not naïve.
It is not unrealistic.

It is already unfolding.

Every healed Black man…
every empowered Black woman…
every conscious Black child…
every unified Black community…
every bold Black entrepreneur…
every emotionally literate Black family…
every awakened Black leader…

is a seed of this future.

Claiming a future requires courage to be seen as we are becoming. Growth often disrupts comfort. It challenges expectations, both external and internal.

But expansion always does.

Black America has expanded before. Each expansion brought new responsibility, new possibility, and new identity. This moment is no different, except in scale.

The scale now is global.
The scope now is generational.
The impact now is transformational.

The next century belongs to us because we are finally becoming the kind of people who can claim it — with clarity, courage, creativity, unity, consciousness, and joy.

We are not waiting for the world to change.
We are changing ourselves —
and that is how the world changes.

The future is not approaching.
It is already rising within us.

And perhaps the most beautiful truth about the next 100 years is this: **we are not beginning from scratch.** We are building on centuries of brilliance, courage, innovation, spiritual depth, artistic genius, and intellectual power that have always existed within us. The future does not begin in some distant possibility — it begins in the consciousness we are cultivating *right now.* Every choice we make today becomes the blueprint for the generations who will follow our footsteps long after we are gone.

The next century of Black evolution will not be defined by what was done to us, but by what we choose to create. We are standing at the intersection of divine inheritance and human intention. On one side is everything our ancestors endured, dreamed, prayed for, and preserved. On the other is everything our future selves are calling us toward — a vision of wholeness, connection, abundance, innovation, and limitless possibility.

What makes this century so different is the **alignment** between three forces:

- **A healed generation** capable of deeper emotional intelligence than any before it.

- **A technologically empowered generation** capable of global influence with a single idea.

- **A spiritually awakened generation** capable of creating from identity rather than insecurity.

When healing, technology, and consciousness converge, a people evolve.
And Black America is evolving rapidly.

Imagine a future where the brilliance of our artists, healers, scientists, entrepreneurs, and educators is not fragmented but integrated. Imagine a cultural ecosystem where creativity fuels economics, spirituality fuels leadership, and emotional wellbeing fuels community. Imagine a world in which young Black children grow up knowing there is no field where they cannot excel, no dream too big, no gatekeeper powerful enough to block what was divinely placed within them.

Imagine a future where "Black excellence" is no longer a phrase —
because excellence has become the baseline.

Imagine a nation where Black mental health is prioritized, Black
families are emotionally equipped, Black relationships are thriving,
and Black communities are centers of spiritual intelligence and cultural
prosperity. Imagine a world where Black innovators are leading global
conversations in AI, science, tech, medicine, consciousness, and
education. Imagine a world where the African diaspora is a unified
force of creativity, economic strength, and cultural wisdom.

This is not far-fetched.
This is not fantasy.
This is the direction our consciousness is already moving.

The next 100 years will not be determined by systems we did not
design —
they will be shaped by the people we are becoming.
A people who no longer wait for external permission to rise.
A people who no longer limit themselves based on historical wounds.
A people who no longer shrink in the face of fear or uncertainty.
A people who understand that their power is internal, ancestral, and
eternal.

We are entering a century where Black imagination will be one of the
most powerful creative forces on the planet. A century where Black
unity will create global pathways of influence. A century where Black
healing will rewrite generational stories. A century where Black
leadership will elevate humanity as a whole.

The future will not be something that happens to us —
it will be something that flows **from us**.

Because the truth is simple:
The next 100 years are not waiting on the world to evolve.
The next 100 years are waiting on *us*.

And we are ready.

Hope is a discipline."

— **Mariame Kaba**

CHAPTER 23

THE FUTURE BELONGS TO US

A Declaration of Hope, Power, and Purpose

There is a point in every great story when the hero stops running from the past and begins walking toward the future with clarity, intention, and courage. A moment when fear dissolves into faith, doubt dissolves into vision, and limitation dissolves into truth. That is the moment when transformation becomes inevitable.

Black America is standing in that moment right now.

Not at the mercy of the past.
Not defined by trauma.
Not constrained by what was.
But empowered by what *is* and inspired by what *can be*.

Empowerment begins the moment a people stop negotiating their worth with the past. History can inform us, but it was never meant to imprison us. When history becomes a reference rather than a residence, it transforms from weight into wisdom.

This distinction is everything.

Wisdom allows us to extract meaning without carrying wounds forward unchanged. It allows us to say, "This happened," without saying, "This is who we are." It allows identity to expand beyond survival into authorship.

Black America is crossing that threshold now.

The energy of this moment is not reactive. It is creative. It is the quiet confidence that emerges when a people no longer need to prove their humanity, because they are busy expressing it.

This book has been a journey through history, identity, resilience, creativity, healing, consciousness, leadership, unity, and possibility. But above all, it has been a journey toward one sacred truth:

The future belongs to us — because we are finally becoming the kind of people who can claim it.

This is not optimism rooted in denial.
It is optimism rooted in awakening.
It is optimism rooted in evidence.
It is optimism rooted in evolution.
It is optimism rooted in a deep spiritual knowing that our best days have not passed — they are rising.

We are stepping into a future shaped not by fear, but by vision.
Not by wounds, but by wisdom.
Not by fragmentation, but by unity.
Not by scarcity, but by abundance.
Not by survival, but by sovereignty.

THE FUTURE BELONGS TO US BECAUSE WE HAVE OUTGROWN THE SHADOWS

For centuries, society tried to define us.
Tried to confine us.
Tried to diminish us.
Tried to erase us.

But we outgrew every box.
We transcended every stereotype.
We healed every wound they said would break us.
We created beauty out of brutality and hope out of hardship.
We turned pain into purpose and struggle into strength.

We did not simply survive history —
we transformed it.

And transformation is the gateway to destiny.

Outgrowing shadows does not mean denying darkness. It means no longer letting darkness dictate direction. Shadows exist only where light is present. To outgrow them is to move closer to the source.

For generations, the shadows were externalized through stereotypes, exclusion, and imposed narratives. Over time, some of those shadows were internalized. They whispered doubt. They shaped expectations. They narrowed imagination.

That internalization is dissolving.

As consciousness expands, shadows lose their authority. They are seen for what they are, remnants of a past that no longer defines the present. When shadows are named, they shrink. When light is chosen intentionally, they disappear.

This is the quiet revolution underway.

THE FUTURE BELONGS TO US BECAUSE OUR CONSCIOUSNESS HAS EVOLVED

A new awareness is rising within us — an awareness of our power, our brilliance, our spiritual depth, and our interconnectedness. We are becoming more intentional, more intuitive, more emotionally literate, more self-aware, and more aligned with Divine Intelligence.

Consciousness is the foundation of creation.
Change the consciousness of a people,
and you change the trajectory of a nation.

Black consciousness today is expansive, liberated, and spiritually awakened.
And awakened people do not return to sleep.

Evolution of consciousness is the most decisive form of progress. Technology can advance, systems can reform, and economies can grow, but without consciousness, old patterns reappear in new forms.

Consciousness determines how power is used.

An evolved consciousness does not seek domination. It seeks harmony. It does not confuse control with leadership. It understands that influence rooted in fear is fragile, while influence rooted in integrity is enduring.

This is the consciousness now emerging within Black America.

It is a consciousness that understands interdependence. That values emotional intelligence as much as intellect. That recognizes spiritual alignment as a practical asset, not an abstract idea.

Awakened consciousness changes what feels possible, and possibility shapes destiny.

THE FUTURE BELONGS TO US BECAUSE WE ARE NO LONGER WAITING

We are not waiting for permission.
We are not waiting for validation.
We are not waiting for systems to "fix themselves."
We are not waiting for perfect conditions.

We are building.
We are leading.
We are healing.
We are innovating.
We are creating.
We are choosing.

We are writing our own future —
not in pencil,
but in permanent ink.

Waiting often disguises itself as patience, but there is a difference. Patience is aligned action without panic. Waiting is deferred authorship. When a people stop waiting, they reclaim time.

Reclaimed time accelerates creation.

Instead of organizing life around permission, Black America is organizing around purpose. Instead of asking when change will come, we are deciding how it will look. This shift moves energy from anticipation into execution.

Execution compounds.

Small actions, aligned with vision, create momentum. Momentum reshapes culture. Culture reshapes institutions. Institutions reshape outcomes.

This is how futures are built in real time.

THE FUTURE BELONGS TO US BECAUSE OUR UNITY IS BECOMING OUR STRENGTH

Whether through digital connectivity, shared healing, economic collaboration, creative synergy, or diaspora unity, we are reconnecting in ways no generation before us has ever experienced.
We are no longer isolated.
We are interconnected.
We are global.
We are collective.

A unified people are an unstoppable people.

Unity does not erase difference. It contextualizes it. It allows individuality to exist within shared direction. True unity is not sameness. It is coherence.

Coherence creates amplification.

When people move in aligned direction, effort multiplies. Resources circulate. Knowledge spreads. Support deepens. The collective becomes more than the sum of its parts.

This is why unity has always been feared by systems invested in fragmentation.

Fragmented people are easier to control. Unified people are harder to contain. As unity strengthens across communities, generations, and the global diaspora, the architecture of power begins to shift naturally.

This shift is already underway.

THE FUTURE BELONGS TO US BECAUSE WE FINALLY BELIEVE IT DOES

Belief is the birthplace of destiny.
And for the first time in centuries, Black America is beginning to believe in its own future with clarity, conviction, and courage.

We believe in our children.
We believe in our culture.
We believe in our brilliance.
We believe in our healing.
We believe in our unity.
We believe in our purpose.
We believe in our future.

And belief is the force that bends reality toward possibility.

Belief does not ignore reality. It organizes it. What a people believe determines how they interpret experience, respond to challenge, and imagine possibility.

For centuries, belief was shaped externally.

Now, belief is being reclaimed internally.

This reclamation is subtle but profound. It shows up in how children are spoken to, how dreams are encouraged, how failure is framed, and how success is defined. It replaces fear based conditioning with vision based expectation.

Expectation influences behavior.

Behavior shapes outcome.

Outcome reinforces belief.

This feedback loop is now working in our favor.

CLOSING DECLARATION: A NEW ERA HAS BEGUN

The future does not belong to those who are afraid.
It belongs to those who imagine.
It belongs to those who heal.
It belongs to those who rise.
It belongs to those who create.
It belongs to those who believe.
It belongs to those who choose.

The future belongs to us —
not poetically,
not metaphorically,
not hypothetically,
but literally, spiritually, culturally, economically, and generationally.

We have earned this moment.
We have prepared for this moment.
We have evolved into this moment.
We are the future our ancestors prayed for, dreamed of, and died believing in.

And now, we step into it fully.

Unapologetically.
Unashamedly.
Unfiltered.

Unrestrained.
Unbounded.

The future belongs to us —
because we belong to the future.

And yet, as powerful as this declaration is, it becomes even more transformational when we understand what it truly means. To say *the future belongs to us* is not a prediction, it is a spiritual identity. It is a reclamation of something we were never meant to lose: the right to envision ourselves as the authors of tomorrow, not merely the survivors of yesterday.

Understanding transforms proclamation into embodiment. Words are powerful, but embodiment is what sustains change. When a declaration becomes lived truth, it alters how people walk, speak, choose, and relate.

Embodiment is quiet.

It does not seek applause. It seeks alignment. It shows up in daily choices, in private decisions, and in consistent values. This embodiment is already visible across Black America in families, creative spaces, healing circles, and leadership environments.

This is not theory.

It is practice.

The future belongs to us because **we are no longer living as a reaction to history.**
We are living as a response to possibility.
We are living with intentionality.
We are living with clarity.
We are living with awakened consciousness.

This shift — from reaction to creation, from survival to sovereignty — is the turning point of our evolution.

When a people realize that their voice shapes culture, their imagination shapes innovation, their healing shapes generational destiny, and their unity shapes global influence, something extraordinary happens:

They stop believing in limits.
They stop believing in old stories.
They stop believing in ceilings.
They stop believing in what the world says they should fear.

They begin believing in themselves.

And belief is not passive.
Belief is generative.
Belief is creative.
Belief is magnetic.
Belief is the force that turns unseen potential into lived reality.

This is why the future belongs to us —
because we are beginning to believe with a depth, a conviction, and a consciousness that is reshaping everything around us.

In the centuries ahead, when historians look back at this moment, they will not describe it as a period of chaos, division, or decline. They will describe it as the moment Black America awakened. The moment we remembered who we are. The moment we reclaimed our narrative. The moment we healed our wounds. The moment we expanded our identities. The moment we connected across the diaspora. The moment we began building the world our ancestors prayed for.

They will describe this moment as the dawn of a new Black renaissance —
not defined by art alone,
not defined by politics alone,
not defined by economics alone,
but defined by consciousness.

A renaissance of soul.
A renaissance of vision.

A renaissance of possibility.
A renaissance of self-love.
A renaissance of spiritual sovereignty.

And they will say,
"This was the moment they stopped asking, 'What will they allow us to become?' and began declaring, 'Who are we here to be?'"

The answer to that question is unfolding right now.
We are here to be innovators.
We are here to be healers.
We are here to be creators.
We are here to be leaders.
We are here to be truth-tellers.
We are here to be connectors.
We are here to be visionaries.
We are here to be light in a world that forgot its own brilliance.

We are here to build a future so expansive, so luminous, so bold, and so rooted in love that future generations will not inherit our trauma — they will inherit our triumph.

Declarations shape identity when they are repeated, remembered, and reinforced. This declaration is not meant to live only on the page. It is meant to live in classrooms, boardrooms, living rooms, studios, sanctuaries, and streets.

It is meant to be spoken, felt, and acted upon.

It is meant to remind us, in moments of doubt, who we are becoming. In moments of challenge, what we are building. In moments of fear, what we already know.

The future is not waiting to be granted.

It is responding to who we choose to be.

So let this be our final declaration:
The future does not just belong to us —
we belong to the future.

We are its architects.
We are its storytellers.
We are its innovators.
We are its protectors.
We are its consciousness.
We are its heart.

And as long as we keep rising, healing, believing, creating, connecting, and choosing our highest selves…

There is nothing — absolutely nothing — this world can do to stop the brilliance of Black America.

This is our time.
This is our chapter in history.
This is our becoming.

And the future is ready for us.

New eras are rarely announced. They are lived into existence. Often, people do not realize they are standing at a turning point until they look back.

But this moment feels different.

There is an unmistakable sense of convergence. History, consciousness, technology, creativity, and spirituality are aligning. When alignment occurs across multiple domains, transformation accelerates.

Acceleration does not mean chaos. It means clarity.

It means movement with direction.

It means becoming rather than reacting.

CLOSING THOUGHTS

This book was never meant to convince you of something you did not already know.

It was meant to remind you.

Remind you of what has always lived beneath the noise, beneath the headlines, beneath the inherited stories that tried to define Black America by limitation rather than possibility. It was meant to bring language to a knowing many have felt but not always been able to articulate. A knowing that says we are not finished. We are not stuck. We are not defined by our wounds.

We are in the middle of becoming.

Throughout these pages, you have seen evidence not only of struggle, but of evolution. Evidence that Black America is not merely reacting to the world as it is, but consciously shaping the world as it will be. Evidence that healing, creativity, leadership, unity, and vision are no longer emerging in isolation, but in concert.

That convergence matters.

History shows us that when a people align internally, external change follows. When identity stabilizes, imagination expands. When belief shifts, behavior changes. And when behavior changes collectively, the future reorganizes itself around new possibilities.

This is what is happening now.

Not everywhere at once. Not without resistance. Not without setbacks. But unmistakably and irreversibly.

The future does not belong to us because we demand it.
It belongs to us because we are becoming the kind of people who can sustain it.

A people rooted in resilience but no longer defined by survival.
A people who honor history without living inside it.
A people willing to heal what was broken, question what was inherited, and imagine what has never existed before.

That kind of future does not arrive fully formed. It is built moment by moment through choices, values, and courage. It is built in conversations that tell the truth. In families that prioritize wholeness. In communities that choose collaboration over division. In individuals who decide that their life will be an expression of purpose rather than fear.

If there is one invitation this book leaves you with, it is this.

Participate.

Participate in the future through how you think, how you love, how you create, how you lead, and how you choose to see yourself and others. The future is not a destination waiting at the end of time. It is something we step into daily, often quietly, through alignment rather than announcement.

And when doubt arises, as it sometimes will, return to what you now know.

The evidence is everywhere.

We have endured.
We have adapted.
We have evolved.

And now, we are remembering who we are.

The future is not only ahead of us.

It is already unfolding through us.

ABOUT THE AUTHOR

COACH MICHAEL TAYLOR

The Irrepressible Optimist With a Passion for the Impossible

For more than two decades, Coach Michael Taylor has been a leading voice of hope, healing, and possibility. His work challenges outdated narratives, illuminates new paths forward, and invites readers to embrace their inherent greatness and divine potential.

He is an author, speaker, entrepreneur, and self-described "irrepressible optimist" who has dedicated his life to empowering others to see the divine potential within themselves. Having overcome tremendous adversity, including divorce, bankruptcy, foreclosure, and homelessness, he transformed his life through the power of faith, self-awareness, and a belief in *unlimited possibility.*

Today, he is the author of more than seventeen books, including *Shattering Black Male Stereotypes*, *Adversity Is Your Greatest Ally*, *Divine Dialogs*, and *The Sacred Knock*. His award-winning documentary *Shatter The Stereotypes* continues to inspire audiences across the country by uplifting the voices and experiences of Black men who are leading, loving, healing, and thriving.

As a speaker and thought leader, Coach Taylor is known for his ability to blend wisdom, humor, storytelling, and spiritual insight into messages that help people transcend limiting beliefs and step into their true power. His work has been featured in media outlets, universities, corporate organizations, and spiritual communities nationwide.

Driven by a mission to ignite hope and healing within Black America, he continues to champion a future grounded in consciousness, compassion, unity, and personal transformation.

Coach Taylor lives his life guided by a simple but powerful mantra: **Unlimited possibilities exist for anyone willing to believe in themselves, embrace their divinity, and trust the journey.**

For more info:

www.coachmichaeltaylor.com
www.shatterthestereotypes.com
www.jesuswasacoach.com
www.brothahoodofkings.com